'Heart-rending. Heart-stopping. Heart-warming. *Pain, Loss & Desire* offers hope and healing for anyone who has experienced childhood trauma. A must-read.'

Denise Imwold, co-author of *Cut!: Hollywood Murders, Accidents, and Other Tragedies.*

'In this brilliant memoir, Graham shows his readers the unfortunate outcomes of trauma, and the courage to share his stories so others can break their own cycle of abuse.'

Paula Diaco, https://writestoriesnow.com

Pain, Loss & Desire

GRAHAM ROBINSON

Copyright © 2023, Graham Robinson. All rights reserved.

This book is copyright. Apart from any use permitted under the *Copyright Act 1968* and subsequent amendments, no part may be reproduced, stored in a retrieval system or transmitted by any means or process whatsoever without the prior written permission of the publishers.

Cover and interior design © BespokeBookCovers
Author's photo © Olivia Leigh Photography
Edited by Paul Smitz
Independently published by Graham Robinson
First edition © 2023
www.grahamrobinsonbooks.com

Print ISBN: 9780645785401
Ebook ISBN: 9780645785418
Audiobook ISBN: 9780645785425

A catalogue record for this work is available from the National Library of Australia

Dedication

This book is dedicated to my children: Jessica, Kyan and Kaleb. They are my soul.

A child is a butterfly in the wind.
Some can fly higher than others.
Why compare one against the other?
Each one flies the best it can.
Each one is different!
Each one is special!
Each one is beautiful!
Author unknown

Preface

I felt no emotion when my father died.

As a child, I ached for moments of love and tenderness. Their absence left me empty and afraid. Perhaps they were there, but now they are lost to the passing of time. My early years were one of solitude, spending time in the stark beauty of English winters where fields lay blanketed in white, or the summer in the depths of shadowy forests where the scent of honeysuckle hung in the air. In those moments, I was alone with my thoughts and dreams.

The journey of untangling the complex relationship with my father is a haunting expedition into the depths of the soul. It's like navigating through a dark and mysterious labyrinth where the memories are shadowy corners and emotions crumbling bones that threaten to break apart at any moment.

At the heart of it lies a mix of conflicting emotions. On the one hand you feel a sense of guilt, as if exposing the truth would dishonour him. On the other, there is a deep-seated shame that stems from the actions he inflicted upon you. How do you reconcile these opposing forces?

My story is a tale that is all too familiar—a child abused and hurt by someone they once trusted and loved. The question lingers: will telling this story serve as a balm for the wounds, a means to mend the brokenness? The answer is not easily found. While facing the truth is the first step towards healing, the process is not easy and the pain resurfaces, leaving you with more questions than answers.

I share my experience as a beacon of self-awareness for those who have suffered similar traumas. No judgment is cast upon the events, for they are integral to my identity, shaping my virtues and flaws. Amidst the journey, I grappled with recognising the two sides and understanding how my past has impacted my present.

As the tale unfolds, it brings to light the unexplained sadness and longing that has plagued me throughout my life. The void left by a lack of love during childhood seeps into adulthood, leaving a yearning for a love that never came and a legacy of a hunger for love that endures today.

Memories of my father's indifference intertwine with a desperate desire to make him proud, and this deep-rooted need haunts me even now that he has gone.

As I delved into the pain, I discovered how the early trauma wounded my inner child, leaving me emotionally detached and disconnected. An understanding grew that the fault lies not with me but with my father and his history of pain and hurt.

Ultimately, this is a story of healing—a raw and transformative process. It serves as a reminder that everyone's path to recovery is unique and challenging. It's a journey of setbacks and progress, but hope glimmers on the horizon. It is a testament that no matter one's age or circumstance, acknowledging the pain and embarking on healing is never too late. For it is in the darkest moments that the light within us shines the brightest with courage and resilience. You can emerge from a cocoon of self-imposed pain and, like a butterfly spreading its wings, soar into a new freedom.

The events described in this story are true, but names, and locations have been changed.

≠

A child is a butterfly in the wind.
Some can fly higher than others,
but each one flies the best it can.
Why compare one against the other?
Each one is different!
Each one is special!
Each one is beautiful!
Author Unknown

Part One: Pain

Drenched in sweat and dust, the gallant horse beneath him pressed forward relentlessly, obedient to its master's urgent commands. With sword raised high, reflecting the brilliance of the noonday sun, he rode with a grace born of countless hours spent as a youth in perfect harmony with his loyal steed.

In his heart, hatred surge, fuelling his pursuit. The rugged terrain, strewn with rocky outcrops mattered little to him as he fixed his sights solely on his prey. Dust clouded his view, obscuring his enemy from sight, yet he refused to relent. Frustration tore from his lips, whipped away by the hot wind.

The image of his beloved Alexandria emerged before his mind's eye. A love cruelly taken from him; stolen by merciless hands. They would pay for their heinous act, and he swore to take their heads as retribution. Displaying them as a grim warning at the entrance to his home, just as they had done to her. But a bittersweet wish lingered beyond the thirst for vengeance—a yearning for a love he'd never known, a lost chance for a different life, one filled with tender moments where words of affection and devotion could have changed the course of events.

Pausing, thinking of lost love, then, closing the book, placing it alongside the half-drunk cup of tea on the table. Hands in pockets, strolling to the window you're drawn to the beauty of the azaleas glowing in the sunlight, alongside white flowers whose name escapes you. Noticing the dry soil, making a mental note to water the garden.

Your thoughts return to the past, and a tremor seizes your hands, the memories etched vividly in your mind. Forgiveness is elusive and you struggle to find it for a father who had caused you such pain.

In that moment, you marvel at how vividly the past persists while the present slips away almost unnoticed. The book's title is hard to recall, replaced by haunting images of a time long gone, when an emotional terror was carved in your soul.

≠

The dying sun's feeble rays barely touch the forest's outstretched branches. The air is heavy with the scent of damp earth mingling with the refreshing fragrance of pine—mossy undergrowth, slick with moisture, clings to the trees. The forest whispers with the buzz of insects and chattering of birds.

He descends like a storm, crashing through the serene woods, recklessly trampling on the delicate undergrowth, shattering ferns with a thunderous crack that reverberates in your ears. The weight of his presence blankets you, suffocating and stifling. You take a fleeting glance over your shoulder, heart racing, as you dart between trees seeking a hiding place. Breathless, resting your back against the weathered trunk of an aging pine, its bark roughened and mottled like the scars of time. Sinking to the ground, wrapping your trembling arms around your knees, holding tight—hoping against all odds for a miracle. A shadow falls over you. There's no miracle, he's found you.

Heart heavy, you stare at his shoes—loafers he calls them—coated with grains of sand, remnants of that afternoon at the beach, a distant memory now. Ignoring the dampness in your pants, straining to remain focused on his shoes, one with a frayed lace. *Does he know? Should I tell him?* The mere thought tightens your heart, and you dismiss it immediately, fearing the repercussions it will bring. A grunt escapes his lips, and you know you must lift your eyes or face greater consequences. His mouth moves but the words remain indiscernible. Sliding your hand into your pocket, grasping the metallic helicopters that brought you joy now turning to an anguish you don't yet understand. You couldn't resist when you first laid eyes on them. Foolish to have played with them in the car.

Suddenly, his hand seizes your arm, his grip tightens, fingers digging deep into your flesh. He drags you back to the car, throwing you to the ground. His voice echoes through the now quiet forest, sharp and thunderous,

'Where did you get them?' You glimpse up, there's anger in his spiteful eyes. Silence envelops you like a shroud. 'I asked you a question. Answer me or by God...' The damp has become a flood, plimsolls—a fifth birthday gift—darkening with a spreading stain.

You watch him unbuckle his belt, removing it from around his waist, and coiling one end tightly around a hand. He inched closer, the stench of stale cigarette smoke on his breath. The taste of that afternoon's chocolate ice cream turns sour in your throat.

Passing motorists pay no heed to the cream coloured Zodiac idling by the roadside nor the man and the boy—an ordinary family enjoying a late spring day. 'I won't ask you again. Why did you take them?' A pulsating vein in his forehead. Your eyes are fixed on the leather belt. His breath ragged, the corners of his mouth speckled with spittle. He snaps, 'You can't simply take whatever you want. This is for your own good.'

You want to explain, to apologise—but you have no words and deep down you know he won't listen. Pain erupts in your left ear, whimpering, instinctively cradling your throbbing face, a warm trickle seeps through your trembling fingers. Thoughts of running, but a glance at the motionless car confirms your worst fears.

The truth written across your brother's face. Your mother stares straight ahead, unbending. There is no escape.

'Give them to me,' he demands. Hesitantly, reaching into your pocket, surrendering the helicopters—watching in helpless dismay as he hurls them to the ground, his loafers stomping upon them until they are broken and lifeless. 'You asked for this,' he mutters. The belt whistles through the air striking again and again upon your trembling body while you cower, refusing to cry out. His breathing becomes difficult, a wet and rasping sound from the depths of his chest. 'Get... get back in the car.'

Sliding across the red leather seat, you twist and turn in a futile attempt to find comfort. He takes his place behind the wheel, forcefully shifting gears as the car lurches forward onto the road. Your brother looks at you with a fleeting glance, a question in his eyes but his voice silenced by fear. Resting a cheek against the cool glass, trying to quell the ringing in your ears, you stifle a sob. Watching the butterflies flutter among the cow parsley lining the roadside. *If only I were that free.*

Unblinking, impassive eyes, observe you from the rear-view mirror. An understanding takes root: this is not the first and will not be the last time you face his anger. A sharp ache stirs in the pit of your stomach, but the seed of hatred is yet to sprout. That will come later.

≠

A dusting of snow coats the ground, concealing the slush from the previous night's fall. A shrill whistle pierces the stillness, startling the small group gathered around your father. Each shaking his hand, bidding him farewell. You watch from the steps of the carriage, pulling your jacket tighter to ward off the biting wind. Steam hisses from the throbbing engine as it prepares to depart. A guard dressed in royal blue pants with a bold red stripe down each leg and matching coat, marches along King's Lynn platform waving a green flag and calling, 'All aboard.' The year is 1962.

As you settle into the embroidered carriage seat, a faint lemony scent in the air invokes memories of home. You picture your mother on hands and knees, a tin of Pledge in hand, polishing the timber dining table legs until they gleam. The Vicar's impending visit provides an excellent reason to have everything pristine. But you couldn't help but smirk at the memory of the time he'd tried to get you into the church choir to follow in your brother's footsteps. The attempt had backfired spectacularly, leaving the Vicar flustered and red-faced as you sang. But it had gone wrong much earlier, when he tried to get you to wear a white gown. You put it back to front. *How could you tell?* By the end of the first practice, he rolled his eyes suggesting you do something else. *Dumb anyway, boys in dresses singing*. You spent the time waiting for your brother—under the shade of a massive horse chestnut tree in the churchyard, discovering that prized possession, the best conker you ever owned. Maybe God does move in mysterious ways.

Your father boarded as his friends unfurl a bedsheet adorned with the words, *Good luck in Africa, Robinsons*. The wheels' clank as the train pulls away from King's Lynn, picking up speed as the landscape transforms from grey streets to white fields.

Closing your eyes, the rhythmic clack-clack lulls you to sleep and dreams of African adventures with lions, elephants, and other exotic creatures fill your head. Those dreams turn into visions of bare-breasted black women, reminiscent of the pictures in the National Geographic magazines you'd found in your father's desk drawer.

Six weeks later, standing at the railing of the Oronsay as it docks in Cape Town, marvelling at the majestic Table Mountain. The sun's rays paint the mountain's walls in red, yellow and green, forming a mesmerizing mosaic. A passing sailor notices your stare and shares the origins of the mountain's name. 'It comes from the clouds covering it like a tablecloth.' You squint upwards, you can't see any clouds resembling a tablecloth; they are all torn and ragged.

The aroma of exotic plants and bustling crowds in brightly coloured clothes greets you at Cape Town's port, igniting a sense of wonder and adventure. The warmth pushing away memories of England's cold and frosty streets. Yet, as you wait in a sweltering Customs tin shed, the excitement of arrival begins to fade. Men in uniform are in deep conversation with your father, and you recognise the tell-tale sign of concern—the glow on the back of his neck. Holding your breath, you anticipate the inevitable.

The first weeks in Cape Town are spent at a boarding house where the warm-hearted owner always has an array of guavas, oranges, yellow melons, African sausage, and cakes to eat. She offers you a stick of biltong, a popular local delicacy she says, but the taste disagrees with you.

You and your brother decide to venture into the city to watch Elvis in Flaming Star. Skipping along in the sunshine, you feel a sense of joy and liberation that you seldom experienced back in England. In the heart of Cape Town, the dazzling white colonial buildings glisten, creating a picturesque sight. The air is filled with the delightful aroma of red and yellow proteas and frangipanis, but the beauty of the surroundings is overshadowed by an urgent need to find a toilet. Desperately searching for relief, your brother points to a set of grimy steps he believes lead down to a toilet. However, your heart sinks as you notice the sign on the wall, *'Non-Blanke,'* a phrase you don't comprehend. Uncertain and dismayed, you exchange a worried glance with your brother, reluctant to venture down those steps.

With a shrug, he encourages you. Hesitantly you grip the rusting handrail and take the first tentative step. Faint voices and shuffling feet from below halt your progress and your heart races. Despite the unpleasant sweat and mustiness that fills the air you press on, sweat trickles down your back. As you reach the bottom, you're met with the unexpected sight of three black faces peering at you in a mixture of fear and anger. One approaches, his hand clenched into a threatening fist, while another gestures wildly, and raises his voice in agitation, words you can't understand. A hand from the shadows reaches out restraining him. In a rush of fear and confusion you retreat up the stairs, the need for a toilet forgotten. Puzzled, unable to understand the reason for their reaction.

Your brother points to another sign which reads *'Blanke.'* Wary after the previous experience, until your bladder has other ideas and the need forces you to decide between braving the unknown and risking an embarrassing accident. You opt to go down the steps, these are cleaner, an inviting grey and silver-flecked marble with a polished brass handrail. As you reach the bottom, an elderly black man, anywhere from fifty to a hundred and fifty shuffles towards you, hands fussing with a red-velvet waistcoat worn over a yellowing dress shirt. Grey curls lie tight against his head, one leg drags across the floor, clumping with each step. His face cracks into a beaming smile as he offers you a washcloth and a bar of lilac soap.

≠

Months later, your family embarks on a journey to Windhoek in South-West Africa. With suitcases stacked three high on the roof rack, you pile into your father's dirt-coloured 1950 Vauxhall station wagon. The engine strains up the highway out of Cape Town. Pangs of sorrow in your chest as you stare at the Orange River slowly winding its way through green foliage far below. It tugs at your heartstrings, realising that this might be the last time you see the familiar landscape. The lush green of the cape soon turns into sparse grasslands dotted with acacia and baobab trees. Wild animals grace the veld, and you stare at springbok as they prance away in stiff-legged jumps, disappearing in dust clouds. There's kudu and elegant gemsbok with horns long enough to spear a grown man, along with warthog and ostriches flapping their enormous wings as they race away in fright. But no elephants or lions, leaving you with a sense of yearning.

Your father veers towards a village off the highway, where you encounter a threatening mob of men wielding knobkerries. One raises it above his head, gesturing towards the car. Your father slams on the brakes bringing the car to a sliding halt. Swirling dust obscures the view, as it clears, you see the mob advancing, knobkerries at the ready. Your mother screams as your father jams the car into reverse and speeds back the way you came, the Vauxhall engine whining all the way. The men do not give up easily, swinging their clubs at the car. One connects with a headlight; another dents a mudguard.

The years pass, and you find yourself on the move again, returning to England before eventually arriving in Australia, landing in Perth in 1968. Six months later, you move once more, this time to the Northern Territory where you enrol at Darwin High School.

≠

The first day at Darwin High feels like stepping into a hostile atmosphere, one that chills your heart. The school bus ride confirms your fears as you face open hostility. Their pointed fingers and murmurs make you uncomfortable in this new world. But you're resilient;

you've faced challenges in schools before, in Africa, and you'll meet this one too.

As you cross the yellowing grass oval towards the administration building, desperately needing to find a toilet. The school bell rings, and everyone rushes inside a three-story building. Frantically you search for the boy's toilet. The only one you find is for girls, and you encounter two who mock you, laughing in your face before sauntering away. *Where's the boy's toilet?* Humiliated and confused. Unable to hold it any longer, you succumb to the shame as piss soaks your school shorts and socks.

Shoes squelching, you cross the playground, tears streaming down your cheeks feeling the weight of resentment towards every school you've ever been to. Finally finding the boy's toilet, feet jammed against the cubicle door you sit and wait for this day to end. A bell rings late in the afternoon, you hear the chatter of students leaving. With the smell of urine clinging to your clothes you dread the inevitable name-calling that awaits as you make your way to the bus.

The second day didn't begin much better.

'Your name?' the administrator asks, peering over glasses perched on her thin nose. A bird's beak comes to mind and you smile at the thought, but one look at her wipes the smile away. 'Well, what is it?'

'Um, it's, its Robinson ... miss.' You stare at your shoes as if something incredible is happening to them. She lets out a long sigh and places the paper she's holding on the counter. It flutters in the breeze of a desk fan, its blades clicking as it rotates from side to side. 'Your full name?' A hint of annoyance in her tone.

'Oh. It's Graham, Graham Robinson.'

'Graham, Graham Robinson, is it?' There's no smile on her lips. Turning her back, she takes a clipboard from a peg, tutting as her eyes scan down the attached page. 'You're not on the list, Graham, Graham Robinson.' A flicker at the corner of her mouth; she now appears to be enjoying herself. The clipboard goes back up on the peg with an irritated bang. Her hands smooth down an already straight, crisp, pleated top. She frowns. 'How old are you? Do you know your teacher's name?'

Shaking your head, 'No. I'm, um, twelve.'

'Hmm. Go to classroom four. Tell the teacher it's your first day. After that, they can work it out.' The phone rings. Sighing in relief, she turns away and picks it up and with a flick of a long, boney finger, dismisses you; no longer of any interest to her. Wishing you could go home, but you know you can't. You're in trouble there too for spilling milk in the fridge. *As if that was my fault.*

A boy, seated beside a door with 'PRINCIPAL' etched on the glass pane, sniggers. The woman throws a cold glance in his direction and covers the mouthpiece with her hand. 'Quiet Mister Edwards. You're already in sufficient trouble.' Eyes narrowing, he looks at you and mouths. *Watch yourself Graham, Graham Robinson.* You sense that name is going to stay with you for some time.

Hurrying to find your classroom, a male voice echoes through an open window. He's reciting names, and you hear muffled replies in response. Not wanting to interrupt, you look around for somewhere to wait. One boy is not in class. He sits on a bench, skimming stones across the bitumen-patched playground. Perhaps he'll know which classroom you should be in.

He raises an eyebrow. 'Over there, I think.' Indicating with his chin a series of playing fields, but there were no buildings in that direction. Bending down, picking up another pebble, he hurls it against a wall, where it disintegrates into tiny shards.

'Why aren't you in class?'

He grins. 'Don't like school.' Delighted, you decide to join him and pick up a stone to copy his throw. As it leaves your hand it bounces once then stops. He laughs. 'I'm Larry. Are you new?' Nodding, telling him about the boy near the principal's office. 'Ah, Edwards. Yeah, he's a prick.

His old man's important, so he acts like he is too. Stay away from him.'

The school bell rings. Jumping to your feet, you look around. 'My classroom, I betta go find it.' Shrugging, Larry murmurs, 'I'm going into town if you wanna come.'

Kids, yelling and laughing race down the stairs and onto the playground. In the distance, Edwards stands tall, a reminder of the challenges that await you. As you shoulder your bag and glance once more in his direction, you hope to go unnoticed, knowing that avoiding him might be your best chance at survival. With your heart pounding, you decide to follow Larry, escaping from the pressures of school, if only for a little while.

≠

As you clutch the newly purchased comics against your chest, and savour the Violet Crumble bar in your hand, a sense of apprehension washes over you hearing the unmistakable click-clack of playing cards fastened to bicycle spokes approaching. The sound raises the hairs on your neck, it means trouble. You knew who it was, you'd seen them at the shops. Glancing around, you calculate your options, wondering if you can make it across the open patch of ground before they see you. But deep down you know that would only postpone the inevitable.

Edwards appears on his bike, pedalling past with a sense of authority that sends chills down your spine. He turns his bike in a dramatic slide, blocking your path, trapping you. Your stomach churning, the taste of bile in your mouth. He confronts you with a scowl, and demands to know why you're on his street. Mumbling a retort that it wasn't his street, you couldn't help but notice his awkward, gawky demeanour. Freckles dot his long face, and his limbs move without coordination.

'What? What did you say?' Dismounting, letting his bike drop to the ground, raising puffs of dust around his feet. This is the nearest he's been to you since that first day. Standing there, you realise how much taller he is than you. The top of your head barely reaches his chin. Like him, you're skinny, but you're told you have nice blue eyes. They don't appear to have much of an effect on Edwards. 'Hey! I'm talking to you, Graham, Graham Robinson.'

A red-haired boy pulls up alongside, puffing and wheezing. Gathering his breath, he shouts, 'Yeah Robinson. He's talking to you.'

'Shut up, Harold.' Harold pulls a face but says nothing more. His bike wobbles underneath him. Edwards moves closer. 'Robinson. What are you holding in your hand?' Grabbing them, shouting, 'Comics, what a baby.'

A mousey squeak out of Harold as he anticipates fun. His bike tips over, toppling him to the ground. Bouncing up, he brushes the dirt from his knees and snorts. 'He's a baby. You tell him.' Edwards rolls his eyes.

He scoffs at the Archie comic, tossing it away with disdain. The wind catches it and carries it, fluttering like a wounded butterfly, before it drops to the ground and rolls, end over end in the dirt.

'They're mine, give 'em back.'

Edwards ignores you, 'I might keep this one. That's okay, isn't it, Robinson?' He's holding the reason you'd gone to the comic store—the new *Fantastic Four*. It now seemed insignificant.

Harold, lurking in the shadows, creeps up behind you as Edwards steps in your direction. The overpowering scent of liniment fills your nostrils, evoking memories of gym sessions at school, a stark contrast to Edwards, who you'd never seen engaged in any athletic activity other than bullying.

'Are you gonna do something about it?' He taunted, his hand slamming into the centre of your chest, sending you stumbling back into Harold's unwelcome arms. With a forceful shove, he thrusts you back towards your tormentor, an eerie grin spreads across Edwards face. Baring his teeth like a predator ready to strike, he growls menacingly, 'You wanna fight? Huh? Do ya?' And before you can react, his fist crashes into your stomach, leaving you gasping and doubled over in pain. The world spun as you drop to your knees struggling to regain your breath.

'Stay out of my way, or you'll get more,' he threatens, his words dripping with malice. As if that weren't enough, he raised his foot and stomped down on your hand.

As you lie helpless on the ground, ears filled with the fading sounds of bicycle wheels clicking and clacking, Harold's parting words echo in your mind, a warning. 'Do what he says, or else.'

The pain in your body is nothing compared to your searing anger. Thoughts of revenge stir as you nurse your wounds. Murder gnawing at your heart. But it wasn't the first time you'd faced a bully.

≠

As you enter the classroom, the familiar dread washes over you like a heavy, dark cloud. Bullying was nothing new, but this time, it's different. Mister Hendriks, the woodwork teacher, is notorious for his sadistic pleasure in inflicting pain, especially on English boys like you.

The school, on the outskirts of Windhoek, was frequented by Boer families who sent their children there during the week and brought them back to their farms on weekends. Among the toughest of the lot were Harry and Cecil, who had made it their mission to make your life miserable. But even they pale in comparison to the cold-hearted torment that Mister Hendriks unleashes.

In Afrikaans, he bellows, an accusing finger pointing at you, a surge of anxiety in your chest. Your heart pounds as you struggle to understand what he wants.

'Antwoord die vraag,' he shouts again, demanding an answer to a question you can't grasp. 'Speak up, boy? Are you stupid?' he sneers, wanting to humiliate you further. Hoping against hope, you remain silent, praying that his attention will shift away from you. But it's futile. The classroom erupts into snickers and stifled laughter, your misery entertaining them all. His impatience grows, and he gestures for you to approach and stand beside him at his desk. 'Come here, boy,' he commands in a harsh tone. The fear inside grew, but you try to stay strong. 'I ask a question, and you answer, verstaan?' he roars. You keep silent, he revels in his power over you. 'What? What do you say?' he mocks, taunting you, holding one ear pretending he's deaf. The laughter intensifies, and you feel a knot form in your throat.

'Yes ... yes sir,' you manage to utter, hoping it will appease him somehow, more snickers around the classroom.

His eyes scan the room, and a silence settles among the class. You feel like a trapped animal, surrounded by hostile faces. 'Goed,' he says, then he repeats the question, once again in Afrikaans. Your mind is blank, you stare at the sea of unfriendly eyes, each pair glad it isn't them facing his wrath. 'You not answer,' his face crimson with anger.

You swallow hard, 'I don't understand Afrikaans, sir.' The admission fuels his rage, and the mocking looks from your classmates intensify.

'If you live here, you need to learn to speak our language, ja?' he scolds, as if it were your fault for not knowing. 'I will help you learn,' he declares, thick, calloused fingers reaching for your inner thigh. The pain shoots through you like lightning as he pinches and twists the loose flesh. Clenching your teeth, refusing to give him the satisfaction of hearing you cry out. But the pain is unbearable, and tears well up in your eyes. 'Let us try one more time,' he shouts, determined to break your spirit. But the outcome is the same–you don't understand. As his frustration mounts, he yells, 'Are you trying to be difficult, boy? What is answer?' Before you can reply, he twists again, causing you to yelp and pull your leg away.

Your body trembles with fear and humiliation as you limp back to your desk, the bruised skin on your leg turning a sickly shade of purple. The other boys offer no sympathy. With a heavy heart, you know that morning recess will be another torment, and you wonder how much more of this you can take.

Today is the day, you tell yourself, ignoring the anxiety that swirls within as you trudge home from Darwin High. The past nine months have been miserable, and now, with the dreaded end-of-year report card in your pocket, you know what awaits. The teacher's comments left a cold sensation in the pit of your stomach. 'He can do better. Won't concentrate. Plays the fool too much.' Those words seal your fate, and it's everything your parents expect of you.

Shaking off the feeling, you head to your neighbour's house, Mrs Leits, with a sense of urgency. You've watched her daily ritual of stumbling down the driveway, wrapped in a tattered dressing gown, carrying armloads of empty bottles. The sound of glass shattering echoing up and down the street as she carelessly discards them in the rubbish bin. Then, with a final sweeping look, she shuffles back up the driveway. Your mother whines—*loud music and people coming and going all night. It's not right*. But it has given you an idea.

You reach her house, and with shaking hands take the buff-coloured envelope out of your bag. Your heart races as you check for any prying eyes, making sure that old bag Watson, from across the street, isn't watching. She always has an eye on the street, ready to interfere with everyone's business. Lifting the lid off the rubbish bin, a swarm of bluebottles burst out, flailing your arms above your head, you swat them away. Taking a deep breath, gathering your composure, you're determined to carry out the plan. Another quick check of the street to ensure no one is in sight, then shoving the damning report card under the broken glass and rotting meat scraps. Heart pounding, you swiftly replace the lid and escape home, adrenaline coursing through your body like a river. This will work, you tell yourself.

The anticipation keeps you awake until you finally hear it—the distant squeal of truck brakes and the clatter of rubbish bins. The garbage truck is on its rounds. The thought brings a welcome smile as you drift off to sleep.

≠

An empty Bagot Road offers no respite in the sweltering humidity of a 1969 Darwin night. Lowering your thumb, nervously you chew on a broken thumbnail. Sighing, you know you have to increase your pace, the party at Rapid Creek is calling, and despite the distance, the need to speak to Trevor is overpowering. Sweat glistens on your forehead, but you push on, hopeful that the next car will stop.

A gleaming Holden with chrome mag wheels pulls over as if they read your mind. Black smoke swirls from the exhaust creating ghostly shapes in the damp evening air. Grateful, you hurry towards the car, hoping they'll give you a ride. A young, dark-haired girl leans out of a rear window, her thin face holds a welcoming smile. 'Tired of walking?' she asks. You nod vigorously, desperate to get off your feet. But her expression turns into a cruel sneer, shattering your hopes. 'Then piss in your shoes and swim,' she cackles, as the car speeds off, leaving you in a cloud of smoke.

The party is in full swing by the time you arrive. A girl on hands and knees pukes her guts out in the garden while another holds her hair whispering in her ear. Avoiding them, you hesitate, hoping he's still here or it will have been for nothing—the walk in the muggy night, the terrier nipping at your heels as you cut through the garden, damn thing drawing blood. He had to be here.

Three Dog Night blasts from a stereo somewhere in the house. You carefully step over the spread-eagled legs of a boy slumped in the doorway. His head lolls to one side, mouth open, slivers of drool on his chin, a wet patch forming between his legs. He peers up at you and mutters, 'Fuck off,' then slides sideways, head striking the floor with a *crack*.

There's a blue haze hanging above the packed room. *Where is he?* A raised arm signals towards you, but you ignore it. You need to find him. You don't know Trevor that well. You've seen him at other parties, but haven't spoken to him.

Chants of 'Fight, fight, fight!' come from the rear garden. Forcing your way through the noisy crowd, your gut telling you he'll be there. Two girls grapple with each other on the grass, hissing and spitting like wildcats. They claw and tear at each other's clothes and hair, urged on by the mob surrounding them.

You spot him, his familiar features——the distinct hook nose and sturdy build. Your heart quickens, you hope he offers you the job you know he's got going, a way out of returning to school. But when you wave, he merely glances your way before turning away, leaving you feeling rejected.

One of the girls yells in triumph, waving a tuft of hair above her head. Red lipstick smeared across her face, T-shirt shredded, exposing a breast. She doesn't care. The defeated girl rolls around on the ground, shrieking and clutching at her head. 'Leave my fuckin' boyfriend alone,' screams the winner as she stalks away, a satisfied smile on her face. Laughing in delight, the mob breaks up.

Driven back into the lounge room by the swarming bodies, you search for him. Then an arm wraps around your neck. Fingers clamp on your jaw with an iron grip. A voice rasps in your ear, 'I hear you quit school?' Spittle splattering against your cheek.

'Um, I, how?'

'I hear stuff. Am I right?' His face is inches from yours. There's no clue in his dark eyes as to what he's thinking.

Nodding, hoping he knows what you want. The stories you've heard about him. *Gossip*, you tell yourself. 'Uh, I hear, heard, you were looking for help?'

'What?'

'I hear you want someone to work for you.' Smirking, white teeth flashing as he nods, releasing your jaw. 'I've never ... I know nothing about cars.'

With a slap on your back, he chuckles, 'Don't worry. I'll take care of you.' As he disappears into the crowd, he looks back over his shoulder and mouths, *See you Monday*.

≠

You were no shining star at school, not even an average one. Seven schools in eight years, across three different countries, *that's why I failed*, you tell yourself. But deep down, the truth is far more intricate and fearful.

You don't know how much of your failure at school can be traced back to that fateful day in the forest. The shadows cast by that event mirror the darkness that engulfs you, the beating an echo in your mind. Inside the walls of your home, love was a scarce commodity, hidden away from your grasp, leaving you emotionally isolated. You yearned for someone to hold you close and mend your heart. But the fear of rejection and disappointment bound your lips shut, leaving you to suffer in silence.

Amongst the haze of your time at school a few memories are precious, none linked to academic success. The two etched most fondly in your heart, are, when you proudly captained the B-side school soccer team in Africa. Another when your artistic flair earned you third place in an art competition, a drawing of the Beatles. Sadly, your parents failed to attend the ceremony, an emptiness that lingers.

Yet, the fondest was the day of your first kiss. It was a rainy afternoon when Sylvia beckoned you and another boy to play spin the bottle at her house. The thrill of her parents being away added to the moment.

The bottle spun, teasing as it slowed coming to rest, not pointing at you or the other boy, who shouts, 'Spin again!'

Heart pounding, palms sweaty you watch her take the bottle in her six-year-old hand, you're torn between terror and exhilaration. She spins once more, it slows, lurches, rolls, and comes to a stop pointing at you. It's you, it's you!' the boy cries.

Sylvia, a mischievous twinkle in her eyes hesitates, hands covering her blushing face. 'I've never kissed a boy,' she whispers.

The other boy squeaks, 'You have to. You said.'

Sylvia stutters, 'I ... I ... I can't.'

'You said. You said,' he repeats.

You remain silent, with mixed feelings of terror and delight. Sylvia suggests that you retreat into the cupboard under the stairs. Meekly following as she opens the door, ducking her head and going inside. Light seeps through a crack beneath the closed door. She sits, legs crossed, eyes shimmering with uncertainty. 'Do you want to?' she asks, her voice low.

Nodding, your throat tightens as she leans closer. Lips meet, and you can feel your heart doing somersaults. Her lips are soft. But you pull away, unsure of what to do.

Disappointment in her voice as she questions you, 'Don't you like me?'

'I do. I'm, I'm just...' Your words trail off as you sit numbed by your emotions.

She leans in again, eyes closed, once more her lips meet yours. That moment is an awakening and an experience that will shape your path in ways you can't yet comprehend.

≠

As you set out on your first day of work, at thirteen, the world stretches before you like an unexplored landscape, yet you are unaware of the shadows that lie ahead. Instead, you are brimming with excitement. Smiling, convinced that this will be what you need. The smile disappears an hour later in the relentless heat and humidity. Your shirt clinging uncomfortably to your back, perspiration across your brow. Despite the discomfort, you are determined, knowing that the workshop is not much further.

As you turn a corner, you encounter a woman seated on a flimsy plastic chair in front of a laundromat. The chair bottom grazes the pavement. Her eyes hold indifference as she briefly glances at you before returning to the magazine resting on her lap. She lights a cigarette, and a raspy cough shakes her large frame. Hawking up phlegm she spits it out near your foot. Holding back a grimace, you cross the road to Haan Auto-Electricians.

Approaching, you hear the sharp sound of scraping metal piercing the air, coming from a car on the street with a raised hood. Two legs in blue King Gee shorts, the body hidden, hunch over a mudguard. Uncertain whether to call out, you cough, hoping for a response. No acknowledgment, so you try again, louder. The figure in the blue shorts turns, and Trevor emerges. A fleeting recognition passes across his face, and he retreats back under the hood.

'Shit, Haan, it's that kid I told you about.'

Another face appears, this one resembling a withered apple core, he peers at you from the other side of the car. Striking blue eyes, scrutinize you. His voice has a guttural accent, making him hard to understand.

'Do vat Trevor say,' he utters before vanishing back under the hood, the scraping sounds resume.

There's a mix of eagerness and curiosity as Trevor leads you into the workshop. 'Did you tell your parents you're going to work here?' Wiping his hands on an oily rag.

Pausing, recalling the conversation with them. Your father's finger pointing at your chest, his words spat at you like venom. 'What? What ... do you mean? You're not going back to school? Who the hell are you to tell us what you'll do?'

'Umm, there's ... I ...'

His hands clench as he gathers his breath. 'You'll do what we tell you. You're not leaving school and that's final!'

Petulantly, stamping your foot, shouting, 'I can. If I wanna. I got a job, so there.'

Leaning forward, he lowers his voice. 'No, you can't sonny. If you don't go to school, you won't live under my roof.' The walls rattle as he slams the front door. Your mother shakes her head, eyes filled with disappointment.

'Yeah. They think it's great.'

'Good. C'mon, let me show you around.'

As you enter the workshop, you notice a blackened timber bench stretching across the rear wall. Tools of all shapes and sizes lie scattered across its surface. In the centre stands a hoist. Suspended from it, a peach Volkswagen Kombi. The glow of the workshop's overhead lamps shimmer on the paintwork. You find yourself irresistibly drawn to the Kombi. Your fingers reach out to run along the smooth body. Before you can make contact, Trevor shouts, 'Keep your hands off!' He takes your elbow, leads you away, and explains, 'That's the boss's car.' As you turn away, you can't help but steal one more glance at the Kombi. Trevor continues, 'Over there's his office.' Pointing to a timber-framed glass cubicle, an old desk scratched and scarred the only furniture, other than two rusted metal chairs. Above the door, a calendar from 1968 with a picture of Miss December holding a drill across her breasts. 'There's a shithouse and storeroom out back.' He winks, 'I'll show you them another day.'

'What can I do?'

'What can you do? Good question,' he replies, smiling and playfully punching you on the arm. 'Start by cleaning these.' Pointing at the grease-covered tools on the bench, 'I need them done right away. There's a sink near the storeroom and kerosene. Scrub and rinse 'em, showroom good.' With that, he walks away, hands in his pockets, whistling tunelessly.

Weeks pass, and you grow tired of cleaning tools and greasing bearings. You want to work on a car. Tentatively, you suggest this to Trevor.

He snaps, 'Clean the damn tools as I asked. That's all you're good for.' Protesting, until he holds up a hand. 'I'd watch myself if I were you. If you don't like it, you can always leave.' You shut your mouth. Trevor laughs. 'Don't look so serious. C'mon, help me with these,' pointing at massive bearings lying on the bench. 'The lubricant is in the storeroom.'

Entering the storeroom is rare, as he usually keeps it locked. As you step past him you feel his hand on your back, and with a violent shove he pushes you inside and slams the door behind him. Stumbling, you trip over a can on the floor sending it slamming into a corner, it bursts open, and black grease oozes out.

Turning to face him, 'What the ...?' Your words choke in your throat seeing the gunmetal-blue strip in his hand. His eyes are menacing as he runs his fingers along its length. 'You need a lesson.' Chills run down your spine. With a cruel laugh he whips the strip across your legs. Crying out, you drop to your hands and knees. Putting a finger to his lips. 'Shhh. Don't want the boss to hear. Jesus, look at this mess.' Shaking his head and tut-tutting, a teacher talking to a naughty child.

You crawl across the rough concrete floor, huddling in a corner, covering your head with your hands, going back to the safe place—the one you found when you were five. Boots thud on the concrete floor. A snigger. 'Where do you think you're going?' The strip whips across your back, tearing through your shirt. His panting loud in the small room, his anger palpable as he strikes again. The strip twangs as it strikes a shelf. 'Shit,' he mutters, dropping it to the floor. 'Betta keep quiet or else, now get back outside.' Fighting back tears, you struggle to your feet, and follow, head lowered.

$\neq$

Standing before a dreary looking grey block building, you try to recall who mentioned the cheap rooms here; maybe Trevor? But the memory remains hazy. The thought of returning home is unbearable—your parents' cold, endless silence amid their relentless pressure about returning to school. Taking a deep breath, you muster the courage to slide open the aluminium door and step inside.

A man, engrossed in the NT News sits behind a small counter. His scowl, as he looks up, signals trouble.

Placing the paper down, he leans forward, 'What do you want, kid?'

Caught off guard, unsure if this is a good idea, you try to sound grown up, but your voice quivers, coming out as a high-pitched squeak. 'I, I'd like a ... a room. If? Plee, please.'

'This hostel is for men. Working men. Not kids.'

'I've got a job and money,' you respond, hoping to convince him.

He brightens, and his face relaxes at the mention of money as he glances below the counter. 'Do your parents know you're here?'

'I, uh, I can't. It's...' you trail off, feeling stupid.

A scratching sound fills the uneasy silence as he rubs his jaw. 'How long do you want to stay?'

'Uh, I've got forty-five dollars.' You hear the desperation in your voice.

'That'll get you three nights,' he concedes. Digging into your pocket, you spread the notes on the counter before he changes his mind. He slips the cash into his pocket and hands you a key, and grunts, 'Down the walkway, number eleven. There's a towel and soap. You got to get everything else you need.'

Relief washes over you as you head towards the room swinging your arms briefly but stop, fearing you'll be mistaken for a child. Three nights is not enough, but that concern can wait until later.

By the second night, earning enough money to extend your stay at the hostel is all you can think about. You sink onto the bed, rubbing the painful welts on the back of your leg inflicted by Trevor, who seemed to take even greater pleasure in your suffering today. Rolling over, *'Fuck him.'*

The net curtains flutter in the breeze from an approaching storm. You can't be bothered getting up to close the window; your mind tussles with how you can get the money to stay. Payday is three days away, and Haan won't let you have your pay early.

Footsteps echo on the walkway. You pay little attention, accustomed to the constant comings and goings. However, these stop at your door, and a knock follows. Your breath catches in your throat.

'Mr. Robinson. You in?' The voice belongs to the man from the office, you swing your legs off the bed, freezing at the realisation that he's not alone, as your father says, 'Knock again.'

Your heart races as you burrow into the bed, wondering if you locked the door. The second knock is louder, you clench your jaw to stop your teeth from chattering.

'Try the door. See if it's unlocked,' your father demands.

'I can't. Once someone occupies a room, we're not allowed to enter.' 'I'm his father. Try.'

'I really shouldn't.'

Irritated, your father snaps, 'You shouldn't rent rooms to thirteen-year-old kids either.'

The doorknob rattles, panic courses through you. With relief, you hear, 'It's locked. Come back later. I'll let him know you were here.'

No. Don't do that,' your father says as their footsteps fade.

Your mind races. Should you peek outside to make sure they're gone? No, that's too risky—they might still be there. Getting more money is no longer your greatest concern as you press your face into the pillow. You'll have to leave. *FUCK!*

≠

'This yours,' Haan says, tapping an envelope on the desk, its edges curling in the heat. 'Trevor says you not need anymore,' sniffing, taking a rag from the pocket of his sweat-stained overalls, wiping his nose, inspecting it, then stuffing the rag back in the pocket. He taps the desk again. 'Take dat. You find other work.'

This day has been a rollercoaster, and it's getting worse. 'Why? I've done all, all he...'

Haan waves his hand dismissively, 'No work. You finish.'

It's clear that no amount of pleading will change his mind. Understanding dawns. Earlier, Trevor had greeted you with warmth, putting an arm around your shoulders, the friendliest he'd been in weeks. 'The boss wants to talk to you.'

Shrugging his arm off. 'Why?'

'He'll be back after two. You'll find out then.' Strolling away, his hands in his pockets, whistling tunelessly as always. Something unsettling about his behaviour like he knows more than he's letting on, and the thought makes your stomach churn.

Haan's indifferent response only deepens your frustration, and you find yourself clenching your fingers around the edge of the cold metal chair, your body tense with apprehension. Catching his eye, he looks away. It's as if he knows what's happening and chose to ignore it. Standing up, you grab the envelope, barely acknowledging him, and leave without a backward glance. The weight of Trevor's gaze follows you, but you're beyond caring. *I don't need this fuckin' job.*

Seeking refuge in a nearby milk bar, you let the reality sink in. The situation seems bleak, and you consider giving up and returning home, for one moment. But deep down, you know that's not an option. There has to be another way. The milk bar's atmosphere mirrors your mood—depressing, suffocating. You sit on the sticky vinyl seat, your bland white puddle of a milkshake mocking you, listening to the radio's blur of sound. You want to smash your fist on the table and shout, it's not fair, but restrain yourself—or you know you'll be told to leave. One rejection today is enough.

Memories of better days flood your mind—times spent with Larry, who was always there for you. How you worked together at a fish-and-chip shop on Cavanagh Street. You went after school and perched on a metal stool in a hot, stuffy back room, bent over a bucket of water and a sack of potatoes, peeling for hours with blunt-edged knives. The owner paid in bottles of Fanta or Coke; you got a few cents for the empties. You smile, remembering those times.

He also helped when you needed to get away from your parent's, letting you stay at his house so regularly that you became part of his family. You remember when they met your mum and dad. *What a fuck-up that was.* Your dad, dressed in his favourite sky-blue safari suit, your mum in an olive-green strapless dress and high heels, as if heading to the opera. They stayed for an hour before making an excuse and leaving. Larry's mum wrapped her arms around you, words unnecessary.

The radio's volume increases, breaking your thoughts, the woman behind the counter singing along. Her cheerfulness contrasts with your mood and feelings of frustration. Downing the last of your tasteless milkshake, you resolve to find Larry, the one person who might understand and offer help.

≠

The pool hall is a dingy, windowless shed. The man who runs it, reputedly from Turkey, wears his shirt unbuttoned to the waist, displaying thick, curly black hair, and a chunky gold chain around his neck, but seeing Larry, brings relief.

'Hey, Graham. How are you?' Shaking your head, you can't speak, fearing tears.

He moves closer, putting a hand on your shoulder. 'What's up?'

The words tumble out. 'They told me to leave at work. Bastards. Also, dad found out where I was staying. I gotta find somewhere else to stay now.'

Larry drops his hand. 'Geez. That's shit. But I'm sure it'll work out.' Turning away, placing his cue back in the rack, he says, 'Hey, guess who I saw last night?'

You stare at him in dismay. *Has he heard a word I said? It'll work out—easy for him to say.*

He lowers his voice as if someone in the near-empty pool hall might overhear. 'Remember the girls, the ones we took to the Star? I saw Paula again.'

As you think back to those awkward moments with Lucy and Paula, you can't help but feel a twinge of regret.

$\neq$

Lucy and Paula, are inseparable friends, and the subjects of Larry's plan. Eager to increase our chances of getting them to go out with us, he proposes asking both girls out together, hoping they'll then say yes.

You approach Lucy and stammer out Larry's message about him and Paula. Your stammer betrays your nerves as you ask if she would like to go to the pictures with you. To your delight, she agrees.

You and Larry buy matching shirts adorned with fashionable pink floral patterns, the latest trend, according to the shopkeeper. You discuss his plan. It's simple—start by holding hands, then proceed with the rest.

However, as the evening unfolds, your courage begins to waver. *Should I take Lucy's hand? Maybe I should follow Larry's lead and put an arm around her shoulders?* Seeing Larry and Paula getting along so well adds to your nervousness. Mixed thoughts race through your mind, your palms damp. As the movie comes to an end, you reach out to grip Lucy's hand, but instead knock over what's left of your Coke. Despite the mishap, you manage a satisfied smile, grateful for the chance to at least touch her hand.

In silence, you walk to the bus stop. As you part, you want to ask if she'd go out with you again. However, the words get caught in your throat.

Later, Larry boasts that he touched Paula's tits. You don't believe it, but the experience makes you wish you'd taken the chance to be closer to Lucy. You hope there'll be another opportunity. There isn't.

≠

Shaking your head, 'What ... I don't care about that. Can I stay at your place?'

'Sorry. We got the mob up from Alice. It's nuts at the moment. That's why I'm here. Alex, he might ...' Larry gestures towards a man at another table. 'He's got a place near the rail yards. If you got money, I bet he'd let you stay.'

'Ya reckon he might?'

Shrugging, 'Can't hurt to ask. C'mon.'

Alex is concentrating on his shot. Watching him, wondering what you'll do if he says no. You may have to return home, a thought that fills you with dread. His cue strikes the white ball with a solid thunk. It goes racing along the edge of the green baize cloth, clips the black, knocking it into a corner pocket.

'Great shot,' Larry says, clapping his hands.

Alex grunts. 'I've done better.'

'Alex, this is Graham. He needs a place to crash. Can you help him out?'

With a raised eyebrow, he looks you up and down. 'I don't run a squat for every kid in town.' He turns away, chalking his cue. Turning back to face you. 'Got any money?'

Excitedly, you nod. 'Yes, got paid today.' Instantly regretting it as Alex shifts his feet, his eyes questioning. You have the four ten-dollar notes from Haan and the money the man at the hostel returned, a one-night refund, insisting you were lucky to get that. Fifty-five in total. 'Some.'

'Okay. You can crash for a couple of nights. It's nuthin' fancy,' he says, putting the chalk down on the edge of the table and jamming the cue in the rack. 'I'm heading there now if you wanna come.' Holding out his hand, 'Give us some then.'

Your stomach clenches. 'How, how much do you want?'

Looking thoughtful, his fingers tease an angry-looking pimple on his chin, 'Need some smokes, umm, petrol too. Reckon twenty will do it, for now.'

A sense of unease in you as Alex navigates the Falcon through the streets. The sun casting shadows over the cracked pavement as you approach the house. His place is in stark contrast to your parent's home. The windows are covered with cardboard, and broken glass shards are scattered on the ground. The peeling paint on the walls adds to the overall shabby appearance.

Inside, it isn't much better. The air is heavy with the smell of musty old furniture and a hint of cigarette smoke. You see a boy curled up on a threadbare lounge.

Alex yells at him. 'Sam. Get up. You can't sleep all fuckin' day.' Sitting up, rubbing his face, blinking like a baby owl, the boy staggers to his feet and shuffles from the room, leaving you alone with Alex.

'I'm not putting him out? Am I?'

'Nah. People come and go. Sam's been here awhile.' He leads you to a corner of the room, to a stained mattress on the floor. 'You can crash on this for a few nights.' His face hardens—a flicker of cunning in his eyes. 'How much money you got left?'

Do you tell him the truth and risk having nothing for yourself? Caught in the glare of his eyes, you lie. 'Um, twenty.'

'Good. Let's get a feed.'

Though grateful for his help, the pit in your stomach deepens as you climb back into his car. You hope things will take a turn for the better soon.

Hamburger aroma drifts through the house and apparently enters Sam's dreams. Tottering into the room, hair tousled, shirt undone, his stomach bounces like a plate of jelly. He sits and wolfs down his burger, meat, bread and beetroot disappearing down his throat. With a loud burp, wiping his greasy fingers on his shirt, he mutters, 'Get any smokes?'

Alex moans. 'Fuck me, Sam.' Flipping a packet of Chesterfields across the table. Lighting one, Sam blows smoke in your direction, then turns to Alex.

'Hey, now there's three of us, we can get that copper.'

Unsure of what he means, not keen on anything to do with the police, 'What do you mean get the copper? The police? Why?'

Spluttering, Sam says, 'No fuckwit. Copper, wire, copper.' Sneering, he blows more smoke in your direction. 'Fuck, where'd you find him, Alex?' Coughing, his face reddens. Taking a deep breath, he continues, 'Tell him Alex.'

Alex, with a humourless grin, 'It's in the rail yard. We're gonna get it.' 'Why?'

Sam rolls his eyes. 'Geez, fuck me. We sell it, stupid.'

Snorting, Alex glares at Sam. 'Shut the fuck up. '

Scratching your head, 'Don't the rail people own it?'

Alex's face darkens. 'No.'

Sam insists. 'C'mon Alex. Let's do it.'

'They're big effen things. It'll take both of you.' Alex's eyes fix on you. 'Are you game, Graham?'

Sam taunts. 'He's a scaredy cat, aren't you? Scaredy cat, scaredy cat,' poking his tongue out. Your throat is dry, but you nod. *What else can I do?* 'I didn't think you'd have the guts. Let's go tonight, Alex. Please,' Sam begs.

'I'm gonna get some sleep. I'll decide later.'

Sam spends the afternoon pacing up and down, opening cupboard doors, then in frustration slamming them shut again. Sits, gets up, and then sits. Alex yells from the bedroom, 'For fuck's sake, stop the goddamn noise.'

Sam, irritated, shouts back, 'I'm getting ready.'

'There's nothing to get ready. Shut up or I'll smack you one.'

Crestfallen, Sam sits alongside you. *This is going to be a long afternoon.*

As evening falls, Alex reappears and decides that it's a good time to get the copper. As you get back in his car, you're convinced that staying with Alex is not a good idea. The Falcon slides sideways in the dirt heading out of his yard and onto the tarmac, wheels spinning. A hundred yards from his place, Alex turns onto a dirt track, bush either side, the headlights sweep across disused goods carriages choked with grass and weeds. Braking to a stop facing a creaking wire fence, swaying back and forth. You study it, wondering how long before it will collapse.

'You can climb over here,' Alex says.

In disbelief, you look at him, then at the fence, then back at Alex. Sam isn't saying a word. 'You sure?'

'Yeah. The copper's right in front once you're over.'

How he knows this, he doesn't say. The fence continues to creak. Shaking your head, not wanting to climb the fence or search the bush at night for bloody copper, 'How'll we know if we find it?' '

They're rolls of copper wire. There won't be anything else lying on the ground, will there? I'll leave the lights on. Hurry up, before someone comes.'

Snakes, rats, there are plenty of things on the ground. As you turn to tell him, he lashes out with the back of his hand, striking you across the lips, the taste of blood filling your mouth. 'Go and fuckin' find them before I do some real damage.'

Holding a hand against your lip, you get out. Sam is waiting. You see him shaking; you guess he doesn't want a smack across the face.

The sound of purring engines carries across the rail yard from the cars on the Stuart Highway. You approach the fence; Sam holds back. Taking a firm grip, it wobbles, glancing back at the car, you know Alex is watching your every move. Placing a foot on the fence, it begins to dip and sway, and you pause, waiting for it to stop. Then, deciding all you can do is move forward, you reach up for another handhold. The fence buckles, but you're committed. At the exact moment you lift your foot to go higher, Sam decides to join you. It's too much for it, and with a squeal it doubles over under the weight of the two of you, collapsing with a sharp crack, throwing you both head over heels into the rail yard.

Gradually, regaining consciousness, your surroundings hazy, your head pounding. Blinking several times, you struggle to piece together what happened. You make out the twisted remains of the fallen fence and the rail yard stretching out before you. Sitting up, you try to shake off the dizziness. The taste of blood remains in your mouth. Straining your eyes; you see something nearby that seems to fit the description.

Sam lies beside you, groaning and rubbing his head. 'What happened?' You'd like to punch him in the head to give him something to groan about.

Rolling over onto your hands and knees, you begin to crawl forward, stopping every foot to test the ground ahead. A rustling in the scrub makes you freeze, but whatever it is melts into the night. Shuddering, you continue on all fours; all you want to do is get this over with. Your hand brushes an object. *Could it be the copper?* Tentatively tracing along its length, you feel a thick hard rubber coil.

Sam crashes through the scrub and drops alongside like a baby elephant, mumbling, 'Shit, didn't see you.'

'Looks like we found it,' you mutter, motioning towards the rubber coils. You glance over your shoulder, half-expecting Alex to show up at any moment. You breathe easier seeing him silhouetted, motionless behind the wheel. *What if I go back without the copper?* Rubbing your lip, you think that's not a good idea, unless you want another smack in the face. Suddenly, the car lights go out.

Sam whispers. 'He's turned the fuckin' lights off.'

'You noticed. Got a torch?'

'Did you see me carrying a fuckin' torch?' He mutters something else you can't make out, then lets out a low whistle. 'Is this it? Patting the rubber-covered coil.

'Um, what do you think?' Shaking your head. 'No, don't answer that. What are we gonna do?'

Sam sticks his head up and shouts in the direction of the car, 'Switch the lights on Alex.' There's no response, and no lights.

'These things are huge, too big to move. Have you or Alex seen them before?'

'Don't be stupid. We can't come here during the day. It's private property. Alex said he had.' Sam rubs his head. 'Could we drag them?'

'No, they're too big.'

Headlights sweep across the yard as a second car pulls up.

Sam whispers, 'Shit, someone else is here.' Car doors slam and there's raised voices. 'Alex will get rid of 'em.'

A torch beam pierces the darkness. A faint creak as someone steps on the fence. Sam, inches closer, 'They're coming this way.' Then, without uttering another word, springs to his feet and dashes toward the nearby highway. Even a fleet-footed greyhound would have struggled to match him.

A voice erupts from behind, shouting, 'Hey you, stop!' and gives chase.

You realise it's time to make your escape and bolt in the opposite direction, pushing yourself to your limits. Your footing betrays you in the dark, and you hurl headlong into a concrete drain. Cheek and knees scrape on the edge—gasping for breath, remaining motionless at the bottom, hoping you're not discovered.

A voice close by grumbles, 'One ran this way. Don't know what they expect to find.' A muffled voice responds. The torchlight plays across your upturned face in the murky drain. 'C'mon, get out of there, idiot.' You muster up the strength to drag yourself over the edge of the drain, your legs trembling with exhaustion.

'That's him,' Alex says, stepping into the light of the torch.

You gawk, dumbfounded. 'He's the one who told us to do it,' pointing at Alex. 'He wants to sell it.' '

You piece of shit. I don't know you.'

'That's enough. You can both come with me.' The man turns to you. 'How old are you, son?'

'Um ...'

'C'mon, I don't have all night.'

'Thirteen.'

'Righto. I'll contact your parents and get them to meet us at the station.'

Your heart stops. *No!*

As you head home from the police station your father remains silent. The air inside the car tense. The officer's stern warning about trespassing on private property and the suggestion to change your circle of friends on your mind. You trudge to your bedroom, heart sinking with the realisation—you were now stuck in your parent's home until you could find another job. But, when you thought luck had deserted you, fate intervened, and a week later you stumbled upon a job as an offsider delivering fresh baked bread. The early hours meant you escaped awkward conversations with your parents. However, you couldn't comprehend the storm about to sweep into your life.

The crisp twenty-dollar notes in your pocket send a surge of excitement through you, making you feel invincible. With a confident swagger, you make your way towards the Vic Hotel, anticipation bubbling, eager to meet your friends.

Even at thirteen, getting into a pub in Darwin is not a problem. The Vic isn't as easy as the Parap or the Seabreeze—you've been to all three.

It's Friday and the Vic is alive with the usual mix of people. Office workers mingling with sweaty labourers, happy to escape the day's blistering heat. And then there were the hippies, carefree and uncaring about what the locals thought of them. Their presence fascinated you, as did the girl in the flowing skirt and midriff top, dancing with such abandon, seemingly transported to another world by the music playing in her head. Her untamed spirit, unshaven armpits, and the feather band around her head made her stand out, even in this crowd. You couldn't help but admire her zest for life, a quality you felt lacking. The locals didn't like the hippies, they called them bludgers, not to their face. But you envy their love of life and how they laugh out loud, not caring who hears. They're independent and light-hearted, all the things you aren't. Still, you act like the locals so you don't become the target of scorn.

You find your friends at the rear of the beer garden. Roger and his brother Greg, a rough-looking man, with an unmistakable odour from his work on prawn trawlers. Roger was a year ahead of you in school, he's big, and plays front-row forward for a local League team. They're with two strangers, a girl and an older man. The girl has her arm draped around the man's shoulders, their heads close together, whispering like lovers. They both glance up as you join them. The man has a scar on his face, a slash from cheek to lip, his clothes are patched and stained. You sit beside the girl, her eyes hold a glimmer of curiosity as she runs her tongue over cracked lips and sticks out her hand, in a husky voice, 'Hi ya. I'm Suzy.'

Smiling, you reach over to take the offered hand, but before you can, the man leans across and wrenches her arm back. 'Behave, bitch.' Yelping in pain, she retreats, casting her eyes downward.

Greg seems indifferent, immersed in his beer, while Roger has already vanished, leaving without a word. 'Wanna beer?' Greg asks, placing an empty on the table among a litter of others. 'Hope you've got money. We're out.'

'A little.'

Giggling, Suzy says, 'Great.'

Leaning across the table, Greg holds out his hand. 'I'll go and get you one and one for me.' He laughs as he heads to the bar, patrons giving him a wide berth.

An hour passes. Greg is slumped in his chair, head on chest. You want to talk to Suzy, but her eyes narrow and she turns away to face the older man, the two continue whispering to each other. Suzy sniggers, pats the man on the cheek, says something under her breath, then steals a quick look at you and nods. Breaking out in a bout of coughing, her chair rocks back and forth. Grasping the arm, holding it steady until her coughing subsides. She mouths a *Thanks*, her teeth, uneven and discoloured. With a sniff, she leans forward, arm pressing against yours. A fire stirs in you.

'You got a guurrl fruund?' Blushing, you turn away. The man's eyes dart back and forth between the two of you. Suzy, with a drunken giggle, 'Would you like one?' Bursting into another bout of coughing, and then spitting on the grass between her feet, 'That's betta. Well, do ya?'

The man glares. Suzy ignores him as she reaches across the table, picking up a cigarette pack, giving it a shake, grumbling, 'Shit, it's empty. Fuck, I need a smoke. I got sum in my room.' Winking, nudging you. Your heart races.

There's a thump on the table, as the man thrusts his chair back and storms off, elbowing people out of the way who aren't quick enough to move. Suzy places a hand on your leg, giving it a squeeze. You jerk away in surprise, glancing around in case the man comes back. Her face crumbles. 'Aww. Don't you like me?'

Stuttering, 'I, um, I um ...'

Her hand rubs your leg, she notices your glances. 'Fuck him,' she says, 'C'mon, it'll be fun.' Her hand takes yours as she leads you to the back of the hotel and up the stairs. Pausing at the top, 'You alright?' Powerless to speak, your throat constricted, you nod. 'Good, I hope this is working.' She grabs your groin and squeezes.

The atmosphere inside the room is stifling, the oppressive heat clinging to everything. The ceiling fan's lazy rotation only serves as a reminder of its ineffectiveness. The air is heavy with anticipation, and tension.

As she turns to face you, her tongue peeking between her teeth, a mixture of sadness and confidence in her gaze. She slowly peels the straps of her dress away, allowing it to drop to the floor. Your knees tremble with excitement and nervousness, threatening to give way beneath you. You are caught off guard, overwhelmed by the moment. It's the first time you've seen a woman naked, apart from that night you saw your mother running out of the bathroom to get a towel from the linen cupboard, and your father yelling from the bathroom for her to hurry up. You quickly squash that vision.

Her body tells a story, faded bruises on her stomach the size of a fist. Her breasts lay flat, like a pair of fried eggs; that does nothing to diminish your desire. You hesitantly lower your eyes, drawn to the soft fuzz below her stomach, feeling a swelling in your jeans. Her laughter, teasing as she covers her breasts and beckons you toward the bed, sliding under the sheet.

Rapidly removing your clothes, you fumble with your belt buckle and blush in embarrassment as you struggle to undo it. Her eyes convey a hint of exasperation. The buckle gives way, and your jeans fall to the floor. Kicking them across the room, you hurry to her side, feeling both eager and timid.

Her touch is electrifying as she grasps your cock, sending shivers of pleasure through your body. You arch your back in response. Her laughter is a delight in your mind as she plays with you.

'Oh, you like that, do you? Well, I like this.' She places a hand on your head and murmurs, 'Do this,' pushing you down between her open legs. In a hoarse voice, 'Kiss me down there.'

Like a puppy you eagerly comply, trying to please her, but as you move down, your nose wrinkles at the smell of sour sweat, stale piss, and something else that reminds you of Greg. Stomach heaving, you slide back up, apologetic. 'I can't. I don't.'

Her lips curl into a sneer, 'Fuck it. I'm going to get a beer.' She dresses swiftly and leaves you alone. In frustration, furious with yourself you slam your hand down on the mattress. The room is now hotter, but the heat is not from the air.

A floorboard squeaks, catching your attention, bringing hope. Smiling, turning to face the door with an apology on your lips, and a promise to try again.

The man with the scar leans against the door jamb. Bloodshot eyes dart around the room, searching for something or someone, then fix upon you. Stepping inside, the wooden door creaks behind him, the rasp of the bolt loud in the silence—his boots thud heavily against the timber floor as he crosses to the bed. A vein pulsing rhythmically in his jaw, a hint of the tension churning within. His hands grip the metal frame, his fingernails are chewed down to the quick.

You break out in a cold sweat. 'I, uh, she's not here.'

There's a growl from deep in his chest. 'I sees you watching me.' His eyes continue to dart around the room, as if he expects her to reappear, then, fix back on you. Desperately you look for your jeans, they're on the other side of the room, where you'd kicked them in your haste to get to her, and he's between them and you.

'I ... I ... is she your ...?'

'She's filth, that's what she is.'

You avoid looking into his eyes. Slipping out of the bed, wrapping the rumpled sheet around your waist, 'I didn't ...'

In the blink of an eye, he lunges towards you, an iron grip constricts your throat, suffocating you, he slams you against the wall. The pain is excruciating, your vision blurs, white spots dance in front of your eyes.

'I don't want that bitch.'

Unable to breathe, you stare into a pair of pitiless eyes, then quickly look away. He releases your throat, his fingers grip your hair, entwining and twisting. His face close to yours, he grins, the scar puckers, pulling his lips into a sneer as he presses a thin blade against your cheek. Pleading for mercy, 'No. No,' trying to hold back tears and the rising panic within you.

'I'll cut you from ear to ear if you make a sound. I know you want it, you little shit.' With a forceful yank, he spins you around, pressing your face into the mattress, once a place of joy, now full of fear. You beg him to leave you alone, but your pleas are brushed aside.

'Please, please don't.'

'You want it.' The blade digs into your throat. 'Shut up.' Forcing your head further into the mattress. A thud echoes in the room as his belt and shorts drop to the floor. Panicking, twisting and turning to be free of his grip, your fingers search for something to hold onto as you try to scramble across the bed. Grabbing your ankles, he drags you back. Hauling your arm up behind your back, rasping, 'Take it in your hand. I know you like it.' He slaps his cock into your hand, screaming, 'Put it in CUNT!' Blubbering, you let go. 'Fuck you.' Kicking your ankles apart, the weight of his body on yours is crushing, as he thrusts himself inside. You sob, defenceless and broken.

Afterwards, you lie on the bloodstained floor, defeated and violated. The room shrouded in darkness, amplifies the torment in your mind. You hear faint, distant sounds from the hotel below, a reminder of another world that feels so far away. A filth courses through you, a palpable thing. The urge to cry persists, yet there are no more tears. You're a hollow shell.

Shuddering, as his presence flashes in front of your eyes. You feel his hot breath on your back as if he's with you now. Spinning around, checking behind, nothing, you're alone, relaxing, breathing a sigh of relief.

Gathering up your clothes, pain ripples through your bruised body. The weight of shame and humiliation weighs you down, knowing that this night must remain a secret buried deep within you, no-one can ever find out or you'll become the laughing stock of Darwin, never able to live it down.

You sneak away in the darkness and repeat to yourself; *it never happened, it never happened, it never happened.* This burden you have to carry alone. Another shudder racks your body.

As the years pass, you grasp that your fury runs deep, growing and festering. It's not solely the abuse from your father, but also being used, discarded, and deemed worthless. This is the core of your anger, which won't depart until you take action.

≠

Stumbling out of the sailing club dance, the cool breeze off Fannie Bay beach whips sand against your cheek, stinging like tiny needles. Your head feels heavy and dizzy from the alcohol as you struggle to get your bearings.

Memories of better days hit you, noticing groups of kids huddled together near the sailing club shed, chugging from bottles labelled Fanta but filled with cheap alcohol. A knowing smile at the corners of your lips. You were one of them a year ago. How things have changed since then.

Your eyes are drawn to the couples entwined under the hulls of catamarans, seeking a final grope before their parents arrive. That concern was far from your mind; your focus is on the night's disappointment and frustration.

The waves crash on the shoreline with a forceful thud, their angry hiss echoing the anger within you. The ocean reflects your mood. Staggering across the car park, drawn toward the beckoning beach. This night had been the first time you'd been out since the Vic.

Shaking your head, pushing those haunting thoughts aside, not allowing yourself to dwell on it any longer. Instead, you focus on the person who'd persuaded you to come tonight—Craig, a friend from school. Sighing, wishing she'd shown up as promised by him. Trusting he was right had proven to be a mistake. You and he were good friends, spending countless hours together, listening to Iron Butterfly and James Taylor. Yet, you differed significantly, he aimed to fix the world's problems, while all you sought was the joy of meeting girls.

Suddenly, a rumbling noise broke through your thoughts. Your name is called from nearby. You stop and turn, a car's headlights blinding you, preventing you from recognising the driver. Vaguely, you think you might have met him before, perhaps at Haan's, but you can't be sure. He calls out again, and curiosity gets the better of you as you sidestep the growing crowd pouring out of the dance.

The night's events may have been disappointing, but something within you stirs with the possibility of this encounter. Taking a deep breath, you make your way through the crowd towards the car, your heart beating faster.

'Hi mate. How the fuck are you?'

Resting a hand on the bonnet, you recognise him as Ethan. He hung out at the workshop scrounging car parts from Trevor. The fresh air and buzz in your head make it difficult to form a sentence, 'Greaa ... great car.'

'Yeah. It goes like a shower of shit.' Ethan's eyes are glassy, obvious even in the weak light, his mouth wide open. 'She's ... she's a Hemi, a beauty.' Larry's brother Alan is in the passenger-side front seat, grinning, face empty of emotion. The car stinks, beer bottles strewn across the rear seat.

'C'mon, I'll take you for a burn.'

Craig yanks on your arm, pulling you back. 'Don't get in. They're pissed.'

Pulling free, you give him a dirty look, blaming him for Lucy not turning up as he'd promised. 'Fuck off and leave me alone.' A voice inside your head says *Don't*, but you push it away. *No-one gives a fuck about me anyway.*

The engine roars with a throaty growl, vibrating through every fibre of your being. With a wild glint in his eyes, Ethan revs the engine, you feel the adrenaline coursing through your veins. Climbing into the seat behind him, you can't help but feel excited. *Who needs a stupid girl, or Craig?* You settle into the seat, the engine's growl resonating in your chest, and as Ethan hits the accelerator, the wheels kick up sand and pebbles, showering the onlookers. He shouts, 'Watch this.'

The car slides out of the parking lot onto East Point Road, but the excitement gives way to nerves. Alan offers you a VB, a gesture you must accept in Darwin. He sticks his head out of the window, letting out a triumphant yell, 'Fuckin ace. Yeah.'

Craig's words linger in your mind, causing doubt to creep in. Your grip on the seat tightens as the car picks up speed, and the passing houses become a blur. You peer over Ethan's shoulder, the speedometer is pinned to the max adding to your fear. Everything flies by, you try to ignore the gnawing feeling that this is a mistake. With a lump in your chest, finding it hard to breathe, you close your eyes, trying to focus on anything but the rush of wind and speed.

But before you can voice your concerns, the sound of the engine changes and Ethan's panicked shouts fill the car. 'Shit. Fuck. Fuck, they're going to slow.'

Your eyes fly open, terror grips you as you see a station wagon with three frightened faces looking back at you. Ethan desperately tries to manoeuvre around them, but a truck is racing towards you, headlights lighting up the interior of the car, horn blasting. Panic seizes every inch of your body, screaming, 'We won't make it.'

The car narrowly squeezes between the oncoming truck and the station wagon, only to spin uncontrollably, leaving behind a smell of burning rubber.

Time slows to a crawl. Every detail etched into your memory like a photograph. Ethan's tense back muscles, Alan swaying, arms wrapped around his chest, the approaching coconut tree—every sensation is heightened by your fear.

BANG! CRUNCH!

Metal screeches, glass shatters, and everything becomes a whirlwind of chaos. Alan's head strikes the tree with a sickening thud, Ethan is flung across the steering wheel. Your head hits the roof, and pain shoots through your body as the front seat crumples against the back, trapping your knee.

As the dust settles, you stare up at the stars, but how could that be? *Where's the roof?* Blood runs down face. There's an acrid smell of oil and the persistent ticking of metal.

Rushed into the emergency room, your surroundings are a sensation of harsh lights and shocked faces as you're wheeled past; some turn away. The dance is a distant dream, as you fade into darkness.

Hours later, sitting on a hard plastic emergency room chair, bandages around your head and knee, your eyelids began to droop as you fought the desire to sleep. *Must work out how to get home.* The police have been to question you, but your mind is foggy, your memories unsure. At least, that's what you tell them. They suspect something, perhaps alcohol, but you remain silent. They leave, with a final look of disgust.

A lone boy is seated at the far end of the emergency room. You think you recognise him, but it hurts your head to concentrate. He gets up and makes a beeline for you.

Anxiously, you watch him, older than you—stout, solid, no fat. But he appears to be carrying the world on his shoulders. He drops into the seat next to yours. Tensing, searching in your memory for his name, *Paul. No, that isn't it. Peter, no, Danny, yes. Danny. That's it.* Out of the corner of your eye you see him study your bandaged knee and head. 'You okay?'

Not sure what he wants, you nod, immediately wishing you hadn't. 'Umm, I'm, yeah. Were you at the dance?'

A quick shake of his head. 'No. I work here. In the hospital. I heard some young people were in an accident.'

You bristle at the reference, watching his face, deciding he doesn't mean anything by it. Your head buzzes from whatever the nurse has given you. 'Are you a friend of ...?'

He stares into the distance, then turns to face you and in a quiet voice says, 'Alan.'

'How's he doing?'

Face drawn he looks down. 'He hasn't woken up.'

Sitting together, both lost in your own thoughts. He breaks the silence. 'Oh, I'm Danny by the way.'

'Yeah. Hi. I'm Graham.' Fighting the throbbing in your head, you tell him what happened. 'Alan. His, his head, he, it hit the tree. It was terrible. He just ...' You trail off. *What else can I say?* The picture of Alan's head striking the tree trunk sends shivers through your body.

Danny exhales. 'Yeah, and the bloody driver comes away with a bruised rib. Can you believe it?'

'He was flying.'

Danny looks glum. 'When will your parents get here?'

'Uh, no, they're not. No, I'm okay.'

'You don't look okay. Use the phone here to call them. The nurses will let you.'

Turning away to hide the fear in your eyes, 'Really, it's okay. I don't wanna. They wouldn't understand.'

'It was an accident, of course they will.'

'I'll find my way home.'

He hesitates, shrugging. 'I've finished work and can give you a lift. If you want, that is?' Remaining silent, your stomach doing somersaults at the thought of getting in another car. 'Did the doctor say you could go?'

'Yeah. He said it'd be okay.' It's what else he said that stays with you. If you'd hit that roof a little higher, it would have taken your head off, he'd muttered as you were wheeled out.

Danny leads the way to a cream-coloured Cortina. Your palms sweat as you enter and grip the armrest, enjoying the feeling of it pressed firmly against your palm. As the engine roars to life, your nervousness grows, and there's a fluttering in your heart.

He brings the car to a halt outside your home. The dark is a saviour as you tiptoe into the house, your feet barely making a sound. Every step is a reminder of the risk you're taking. Collapsing into bed, utterly drained, your body aching, yet your mind races with the consequences you'll face in the morning. You can hear their voices in your head. *What have you been up to now? Why do you keep doing these stupid things?*

You close your eyes, hoping for sleep, but the memories rush in. You see those tiny terrified faces and the most unforgettable image of all—Alan's head hitting the coconut tree. Wide awake, you're uncertain of what the morning will bring.

≠

Pain pulsates through your body, there's a throbbing in your head that intensifies with every movement. A quick glimpse of yourself in the mirror, blood seeps through the bandage around your head, leaving a mark resembling a bullseye. Despite the discomfort, you can't be bothered changing your blood-stained shirt, *I've got bigger problems.*

You crouch by the closed door, listening for any movement inside the house. Slowly, you open the door and cautiously peer up and down the hallway. You step out, staggering, gripping a glass louvre for support. The sight of your hand coated in dry black blood sends shivers down your spine as you once again recall the night's events. With a shudder, reminded of Alan. *Fuck.* You hope he's okay.

You take a deep breath, steeling yourself for what lies ahead, and carefully surveying the length of the hallway. You must make it out before anyone discovers you. With your first step, your knee protests, and you lean heavily against the louvre windows, causing the bandage around your head to loosen, a drop of blood falls to the floor. *Shit, now I'll have to clean that up.* There's no choice but to continue. Voices from the kitchen remind you of the danger.

You reach for another louvre for support, you're drowning in fear, yet you force yourself to take yet another step. Your luck runs out as your mother appears around the corner and gasps in horror at the sight of you. Her hand flies to her mouth as she lets out a blood-curdling scream. 'What? What have you done now? Laurie! Laurie! Come and see this.'

Chair legs scrape on the floor, your father storms around the corner, annoyed at the interruption to his daily ritual of fried eggs, black pudding and bacon. Halting, his mouth dropping open. 'What ...?'

The screeching continues from your mother, she's like a demented cockatoo. 'It's those friends of his. They're trouble. He doesn't listen.' The vitriol in her voice shakes you to your core. Your father stalks forward, eyes blazing. He's five feet five in his socks, solid, broad shoulders, a former army middle-weight boxing champion, and that's who he's now become. His jaw juts out, hands clenched, his voice drips with contempt. 'What have you been up to?'

Back pedalling frantically, you instinctively raise your hands to shield yourself from his threatening advance. The overpowering scent of Old Spice fills the air, mingling with the tension. Then, like a sudden rifle shot, the louvre snaps in two, sending a sliver of glass into your shoulder.

'Don't raise your hands to me, sonny. I've beaten better men than you,' he mocks, his hands curl into fists. But it's not his words that hurt, the look of hate etched across his face cuts you to the quick.

As you stare at him, your heart tears apart. You can't contain the years of anger and frustration any longer. Trembling with rage you find your voice, and without caring about the consequences, scream into his face, 'My friend is in the hospital, fighting for his life, and you don't give a damn about anyone but yourself.' With a heart-wrenching sob, you add, 'Fuck you.'

He leans closer, his eyes cold and devoid of any sympathy. 'GET OUT OF MY HOUSE!' Then, without another word, he turns his back and walks away.

The pain in your chest feels like a knife twisting inside, and you whisper, *'Why don't you like me?'* But deep down, you know it's too late. The realisation hits you like a heavy blow. The love and approval you've yearned for from him will never be. At that moment, you know that you can't change the past and that he'll never change.

With each step, the pain in your heart intensifies, the words of your father echo in your mind. 'Get out of my house.' *Well fuck him, I will.* Passers-by avoid eye contact, pretending to be preoccupied with something on the other side of the street. You find yourself drawn to the bus shelter at Parap, seeking a quiet place, your mind too clouded to think of anywhere else to go.

Collapsing onto the bench, you gag at the stench of urine and vomit. You notice the graffiti on the walls. Fiona's name scrawled everywhere with a declaration of love for Eric, the word 'Slut' has been added beneath it. It only serves to remind you of distant school days, almost forgotten.

With your back against the wall, you ache for a normal, loving family life. That is now a distant dream—letting out a long, heavy sigh, accepting that you must find another place to live. Tears stream down your cheeks as memories surface of another painful encounter with your father.

≠

A lively crowd gathered for the grand opening of the ship's swimming pool. Tradition dictates that the pool's unveiling coincides with the ship crossing the equator. It's a carnival atmosphere, a man is dressed as Neptune, complete with a dazzling emerald waistcoat and a yellow trident held high above his head. Surprisingly, you recognise him as the man who cleans your cabin.

He waves his trident, signalling the pool's official opening. Eagerly, children no longer able to contain their delight push and shove, ready to plunge into the pool. You join in, tucking your legs up to create a spectacular splash as you attempt a bomb. But as the ship rolls, the pool water sloshes violently, causing you to collide with the pool's bottom, the water rushes back, engulfing you.

Panic takes over, instinctively fighting and screaming as hands reach out to rescue you. Hauled up and placed on the pool's edge, gasping for breath, water spews from your mouth. The once noisy crowd falls silent. Wrapped in a towel, you feel embarrassed as a stranger suggests that you should be taken back to the cabin.

Your father walks ahead of you, his back ramrod stiff. Your stomach churns. Stumbling, your mother close behind, mutters, 'Keep walking.'

The churning becomes a gut-wrenching pain as you stand forlornly in the centre of the cabin, water drips onto the carpet. The silence is a ticking weight. Your mother's arms folded across her chest indicate her disappointment, and you fight back tears, hoping your father won't unleash his anger. But as you look at him, his expression remains unreadable.

He takes the damp towel from your shoulders, twisting it into a makeshift rope. The air filled with tension as he raises his arm and whips the towel across your legs, you cry out, begging him to stop. He strikes again, whimpering, you beg once more, to no avail.

Your mother places a hand on his forearm, but he brusquely spins around, pushing her hand away. Turning back, glaring at you, 'You always embarrass us. Now stay here for the rest of the afternoon.'

After they leave, you find comfort in the cool, solid floor beneath you. Tears no longer flow, but the pain remains in your heart.

≠

The relationship with your father is a distant one, lacking the warmth and connection that most children long for. Putting it into words is a challenge, as you hardly knew him. His frequent bouts of anger and the violence he displayed leave their impression. You wish he'd been more predictable, allowing you to shield yourself before his eruptions.

You cannot recall a single instance of him expressing affection by putting his arm around you or showing genuine love. However, there's one cherished moment that stands out in your memory. Even though it may have seemed insignificant to him, it meant a lot to you.

≠

The windshield wipers struggled to keep up with the downpour as he drove, his face tense with concentration, peering through the blurry window. The dim lights of a cafe beckoned in the storm's gloom, and your stomach growled, hoping he would decide to stop. You were pleased that it was just the two of you in the car, even though he hadn't spoken a word since leaving your brother and sister with your mother. As the car slowed and entered the cafe's parking lot, ploughing through puddles, the water splashing against the windows. Entering the cafe, a wave of hot air carries the scent of frying fish and chips. Your stomach rumbles again. He glances at you, as you follow him inside. While there is no smile on his face, his eyes hold a kindness you rarely see.

The cafe is filled with men dressed in grubby work clothes. Their conversation muted amidst the clinking of knives and forks. A blue haze hangs over the room. The atmosphere seemed familiar to your father as he walked confidently through the crowded tables. Nobody paid much attention to a father and his son. One man acknowledged him and with a grunt stood up to pull his chair out of the way, allowing you both to pass. Your father nodded thanks in return.

As you take your seat, alongside a blazing fire attempting to beat back the cold English winter you look at your surroundings. The cafe's walls hung with black and white photos of miners, some smiling, others grim-faced, worn and beaten, a hint of sadness in their dull eyes, all blackened by coal dust. Beads of water run down the wall, seeping into cracks, until they reach the picture frames and then fall, drop by drop, to the floor.

With a goofy grin on your face, you look around, feeling a spark of love for your father, and though it may have gone unnoticed by him, it left a lasting impact on you.

≠

The honk of a car horn breaks through the haze, pulling you back to the present moment. You shield your eyes from the sunlight. Danny leans out of his car window with a concerned expression. You rise from the bench, wincing in pain as you limp across to meet him. The throbbing in your head worse.

'Why are you sitting there?' his voice filled with worry.

How can you explain? 'Ah, a fight... at home,' you reply, not sure what else you can say without breaking down again.

Danny nods, perhaps not fully grasping the problem. 'What are you going to do?'

You sigh, shoulders slumping. 'Find somewhere else to live.'

'My old man's got a caravan. It's out of town, but you can stay there. And I can ask at work if they need anyone.' A smile creeps across your face, the first genuine one in a long time.

Not wanting to endure another incident like this morning's, you decide to get your clothes under the cover of the night. You quietly slip into your bedroom, gathering your belongings wondering if anyone will notice that you've gone. You don't believe they will.

A week later, you find yourself working alongside Danny, in the Darwin Hospital laundry.

≠

Danny hurls the spanner across the shed floor in frustration. 'Shit, I give up.'

You know how he feels. You've both been tinkering under the hood of his Cortina for hours. But neither have a clue about engines. You don't want him to give up, so you urge him on. 'You can fix it.'

'It's a piece of shit. You worked on cars. Got any ideas?'

'Nah. I wasn't there long.' Shuddering at the image of Trevor that pops into your head.

He bangs his fist on the roof. 'I dunno what's wrong with it.'

'If we get it going, we might, you know, the thing you said about the girls.'

He grins, 'Is that all you care about?' Picking up the spanner, he laughs. 'I reckon you've never had a girl.'

You open your mouth to respond, then close it. You can't tell him about Suzy. In fact, you can't really count that night. Sniffing, you turn away to hide the shame.

He recently told you about girls who come into Darwin Hospital from the bush. According to him, they will go with you for a packet of cigarettes or a flagon. You were sceptical, shaking your head at the notion, thinking it was unlikely. When you asked him if he'd done it himself, he remained silent. 'It sounds like bullshit.'

Discarding his cigarette and crushing it under his foot, Danny retorted, 'Fine, don't believe me.' He walks away, but not before suggesting that you could try it on Saturday night. You hurriedly follow after him, secretly hoping he's telling the truth.

That possibility appears to be slipping away as the car won't start. Danny turns the key once more—the motor whirrs. Swearing, he turns it again. The engine coughs then with a roar comes to life. Grinning, you clap your hands.

Cruising around town, you end up at Parap shops, a popular spot for showing off Darwin's hotted-up cars. Danny's Cortina doesn't qualify, as the top of the pecking order consists of Falcon GT-HOs, Holdens, and a Mini Cooper S.

Tonight, there's a commotion outside the fish and chip shop. Tank, as he's affectionately known, stomps up and down the footpath, a sign he's in a dangerous mood. He's known for his love of tight-fitting T-shirts and for getting into fights. He's gesturing and swearing at someone inside the shop, loudly claiming, 'Is he trying to pick up my missus?'

Everyone avoids getting involved or drawing his attention when he's like this. The offender mistakenly leaves the shop, only to make matters worse by telling Tank to fuck off. Tank doesn't hesitate, punching him in the head and sending him to the gutter with blood pouring from his mouth. In response, everyone flees before the police arrive. It's another typical Saturday night in Darwin.

Danny moans. 'This is bullshit. Do you wanna go, you know, see if anyone's there?'

A shiver flutters in your chest, nodding, 'What, what will we do, you know, if they're ...?'

He shrugs, 'Talk to them. Wadda ya think?'

As you get closer to the hospital your stomach tightens. *What will you say? What will they say?* Letting out a deep breath of relief when you see there's no-one there. Glancing at Danny, he appears unconcerned. 'We'll come back later,' he mutters.

An hour passes before you return to the hospital, now with a bottle of cheap plonk rolling between your feet on the floor of the car, and two packets of Peter Stuyvesant on the dash. Your heart skips a beat: two girls, their heads bowed in conversation, sit on the seat. Danny whoops with glee, and punches you on the arm. 'What did I tell you?' He stops the car. 'You wanna go ask?'

Gripped with terror, a shake of your head. 'I wouldn't. I can't.'

Picking up the bottle, Danny strides towards them. He returns a short time later with both in tow. 'Yours is the one in pink,' he murmurs, getting behind the wheel. Taking a quick glance behind you, your eyes rest on the girl in pink. Thin legs and arms poke out from the wheat sack that is a hospital nightie. She flashes you a smile, displaying a mouth full of white teeth, then turns to her friend. Whispering, they glance in your direction and snigger. Your ears burn as he passes them the smokes and matches. They both light up, the car filling with choking smoke.

'Where will we go?'

Danny, gazes ahead, deep in thought, and finally says, 'Somewhere private. What about ...' He pauses, then blurts out, 'Botanic Gardens. Shit. We'll go there.'

Impatiently waiting by the side of the car to cross the road into the gardens, your heart racing. A car zooms past, honking its horn, someone inside waves an arm. *Have they done this?* You enter the gardens and find shelter under a cluster of trees. A noise from the bushes startles you, as a small creature scurries up a tree trunk. The girls giggle, the eyes of the girl in pink sparkling with amusement. She takes another swig from the bottle.

Whispering to Danny, 'What now?'

He grunts and replies, 'Find a place and... you know.' He takes the arm of the other girl, and they walk away, vanishing into the trees. She reappears, jogging back to retrieve the bottle from her friend's hand.

You head in the opposite direction, with the girl in pink following closely behind, her warm breath grazing the back of your neck. You turn around, the wind blows strands of hair across her face. She brushes it away and then wipes her nose before heading towards a large tree, and dropping to the ground. You join her. Neither of you speak, creating an uncomfortable silence. *What should I do?* You reach out and place a hand on her arm, but she shakes it off, opting to light another cigarette instead. The red glow silhouettes her face as she stares into the distance. You return to holding your knees, convinced nothing will happen between you two. She flicks the cigarette into the bushes, where it hisses as it lands in a shower of sparks.

Thinking this might be your last chance, you lean in to kiss her, but she pulls away abruptly. Sighing, you decide to tell Danny something happened, as he wouldn't know any different. Content with that, you lie down, hands behind your head. To your surprise, she leans over and starts undoing your zipper. Disbelief clouds your mind. She pulls you on top with a snort, she's naked underneath her nightie. Your hand brushes the hair between her legs as you try to insert yourself, feeling uncertain about what to do. Pushing your hand away, she takes control, guiding you inside. Your mind races as you try to remember what you've seen and read in magazines. *Why didn't I pay more attention to the words instead of the pictures?* She remains silent, seemingly unresponsive to your hesitant movements.

A tingle in your toes, shooting up your legs, and your body bucks as you cry out, exploding into her. As quickly as the tingling sensation came, it fades away. She pushes you off and gets to her feet, adjusting her nightie as if nothing happened. Your cock stings, but you ignore the pain as you tuck it away. Following the girl, you spot Danny emerging from the trees, walking towards the toilets. Hurrying, you catch up with him.

He grins. 'Get any?'

'Umm.'

'Did you, or didn't you?'

'I did.'

At the urinal, you unzip, there's blood on the tip of your cock. *What's happened to it?*

Danny stares at you with a puzzled look on his face. 'You okay?'

'Uh, I don't know.'

'What do you mean?'

'There's blood. Could she …? Um, has she done something to it?'

Doing up his pants, he scoffs. 'Was that your first fuck?'

'No. Well, yeah, sorta.'

He lets out a hearty laugh. 'You've lost your cherry. Good on ya. C'mon, we betta take em back. Unless you wanna go again.' Shaking your head, you do up your pants, careful to not touch your cock.

Back at the hospital, the girls leave without a backward glance. Danny, smirking, 'How's your …?' You don't reply, but your face creases into a smile.

≠

Danny grabs your arm. 'Hey. Did you hear what I said?'
'Huh, what?'
'Your friend, Pig. You reckon he might have some grass?'
'It's Pug, and he's not my friend.'

In Darwin, if you want grass, the drive-in on a Sunday night is the place to go, and Pug is the person to see. Pug is Adrian, someone you better not dare call by that name unless you want trouble. His arms resemble Popeye's, and his hands can easily crush a beer can. His face is rough, making you wonder if he had some unfortunate accident as a baby. One thing's for sure, you don't mess with Pug.

Your first encounter with him was at Darwin High, where the teachers, in their infinite wisdom, thought it best to put you in the 'difficult boys' class. Pug joined briefly but was expelled for hitting a teacher. The silver lining was that with a friend like him, the bullies backed off.

His prized possession, a 1966 Holden HR. He parks in the same spot, one row away from the snack bar, allowing easy access for customers. The snack bar is a humble building, with a two-storey structure at one end for the projectionist and a red-striped awning above the entrance. In front are rows of canvas chairs. There's also a dirt patch around the corner where locals resolve their differences.

Tonight, the movie Planet of the Apes draws a crowd, as a long line snakes out the snack bar door, showing how popular it is. You locate Pug, and he extends his hand. Reluctantly you take it, bracing yourself for the inevitable bone-crushing grip you know is coming.

'How are you, Pommy?'

The nickname came from school friends. You hoped it would be forgotten after you left. No such luck. 'I'm good, Pug.' Shaking his hand hoping the bones knit back together.

He nods without a smile. 'I hear Alan's fucked up.'

'He's not good.' You want this to be over sooner rather than later. Pug can go from friendly to attack dog without raising a sweat. 'Have you got any stuff, uh, grass?'

He's silent, then checks behind and on either side. You're not sure why, but it worries you. *Is something wrong?* 'How much do you want?'

Nervously, you mutter, 'I don't have much money.'

'I can give you a matchbox for twenty bucks. That do ya?'

The other thing about Pug, is, if you ask, you buy. Don't waste his time. Nodding, taking a step toward him, the twenty-dollar note in your sweaty fingers. He lets out an almighty yowl. Your breathing halts, and thoughts of purchasing grass vanish. Nearby fold-out chairs groan and squeak as mums and dads crane their necks to see what's going on, wondering if this will affect their night.

'Fuck, fuck.' Pug holds the fingers of his right hand against his chest. 'Shit, you stood on me fuckin' hand.' With relief, you hear him chuckle. 'Don't worry Pommy, it won't kill me.' He retrieves a matchbox from his pocket with his uninjured hand, conceals your twenty-dollar note in the same pocket. You hurriedly accept the matchbox and retreat to regain your composure and to breathe normally again.

Later, dizzy from the grass, Pug, still on your mind, his hand stained with blood, Danny's voice echoes in your head.

'Bloody hell. Wake up, will you?' He shouts, shoving you. 'I asked if you wanna get out of here.' Startled, you sit up straight, Danny's face replaces Pug's. 'Well? What about it? Shall we?'

'Um, it hasn't started yet.'

Exasperated, he snaps, 'Fuck. Not from here, not tonight.' Waving his arm in a sweeping motion, 'From this shithole.'

'Go? Go where? How?'

'The other day, I spoke to my sister in Sydney. My aunt's not well. What about there?'

'Uh, s'pose.' Your stomach is doing barrel rolls. 'What about work?'

'I reckon they'll let us go.'

You agree, to shut him up. Lying down again and closing your eyes' hoping Pug doesn't reappear.

≠

Danny ran towards you as you arrived at work, catching you by surprise. 'Hey, Aunty said we can go for three weeks. Isn't that great? His eyes were shining with anticipation.

Aunty is the Aboriginal woman who runs the laundry with an iron fist. She's always dressed in the same sunny yellow smock. Not long after you started, she introduced you to horse racing, one of her great passions, along with her love for cigarettes. It's a fond memory, Aunty leading the celebrations in the tearoom, as Rain Lover gallops to victory in the Melbourne Cup, her HMV radio in one hand and the other pounding on the aluminium table in delight.

'Go?' you repeat, momentarily taken back, struggling to recall the conversation from the previous night. Confusion clouds your mind, your head still aches. But then it all rushed back—the encounter with Pug, his bloody hand. The memory sends a shiver down your spine. 'Oh, Sydney,' Danny nodded knowingly. 'You sure Aunty said we can?'

'Bloody hell, yes,' he responded, with a hint of annoyance as he walked away. Following him, you couldn't help but smirk, even though worry gnawed at you.

'Uh, okay. When?' Trying to mollify him and suppress the growing excitement of leaving Darwin.

'I reckon as soon as we can, in case she changes her mind,' he replied over his shoulder, his mood still somewhat sour. Lately, you'd begun to feel like there was nothing left for you in Darwin, and the idea of getting away thrilled you. Yet, Danny's recent moodiness raised concerns. *What if he abandons me in a strange city?* Such thoughts make you think of getting something to protect yourself, but what?

The idea of having a knife enters your head. You tremble at the memory of that night, never far from the surface, but you push it away. *Where can I get one and what sort?*

No good having a cheap pocket knife that'll break the first time you open it. It must be a knife that scares anyone who comes near you. The thought brings a surge of power into your chest.

As you stroll along Smith Street, scanning the shop windows, pausing at a gun shop. Pressing your nose against the window, you admire the glinting brass and polished timber stocks of the firearms, until a curt gesture from the man inside moves you on. Woolworths was not likely to offer what you needed, but then you remembered a disposal store on Cavanagh Street—a spark of hope, they'll have something.

The disposal store is hidden from view down a dark, narrow alleyway. The interior was no better than the entrance. Illuminated by a fly-covered bulb hanging precariously from a threadbare cord. The puke-coloured glow added to the store's odd atmosphere, accompanied by the scent of mothballs that tickled your nose. You squeeze between rows of camouflage jackets and pants. Looking around, you can't see any knives, only shelves stacked with tents, sleeping bags, and camping gear. You spy a counter. Behind it, a man clad in a grey overcoat, a Hendrix T-shirt underneath, flipped through a magazine. Startled, he looks up as you stop before him. Raising an eyebrow, his sharp eyes lock onto you with curiosity, as if surprised to have a customer. A rheumy mustiness wafts from him as he grins, his breath reminding you of the mangrove swamps where you go crabbing with friends. He closes the magazine and slides it under the counter, but not before you catch a glimpse of a woman in black tights, holding a whip. 'Wha-what—what—you—you want?'

'I'm, you got any knives?'

'Yu-yu—uh—scare—scare—of-of—summit?' He gurgles, and starts picking at a fingernail, as if he's forgotten you're there.

Defensively, you snap. 'No.'

He stops picking and sniggers. 'Okay. Look-at the-these.' A skeletal finger taps on the counter, above a row of knives. 'That-that's-a-goo-good 'un.' He points to a glossy black sheath. 'It's-a-a-Bowie.' Opening the glass case, he picks it up and caresses it as one might a newborn kitten, although you think he looks more likely to eat the kitten whole. His dirt-encrusted fingers trace up and down the blade, one thumb oozes a yellow pus. He places the knife on the counter with a solid *thunk*. Gingerly, you pick it up and hold it in your hand, keeping your fingers away from where his thumb touched. Its weight gives you confidence. 'How, how much?'

'You-nu-need-need-a-kn-n-knife that-that big?' A hooting from deep within his throat. 'If you drop–drop–it–mi–might–cut, cut your dick off.' He sneers. 'It's, uh–five–fifty.'

'Five or fifty?'

His face changes, mirroring the black sheaf. He stares. 'You–you–make-make-fun of me?'

Wanting to get away, 'No, no, sorry, I didn't … it's … How, how much did you say?'

'It's fifty-five dollars.' The stutter has disappeared.

≠

Emotions swirl within you as Danny's baby-blue Volkswagen pulls up alongside the caravan. The sight of the car bumping over the rough dirt road served as a reminder of how long it had been since you'd seen your parents. You knew they probably didn't care about you anymore and that filled you with an overwhelming sadness.

Remembering Christmas spent alone in the sweltering caravan with a dinner consisting of dried ham and cheese sandwiches and a stale pudding. At the same time, you couldn't help but imagine your parents having a festive feast with turkey and all the trimmings. The bitterness within you grew, gritting your teeth at the unfairness of it all. *To hell with them and Darwin.*

Danny's car rolled to a stop, a roof rack held spare tires and a jerry can, his Cortina had been sold months ago. The last straw for him came when it broke down on the way to

Howard Springs to meet a girl. 'Heap of fuckin' rubbish,' he screamed. You never saw it again.

Looking at the bull bar, 'Why'd you put that on?'

'Roos.'

Scratching your head, you consider for a moment. 'You expecting to hit one?'

Ignoring you, he looks at the bag at your feet, 'You know we're going for three weeks.'

You shrug, reaching for the boot. 'It's all I got.'

Laughing, he points to the front of the car. 'The engine's in the back, stupid. Some mechanic you are. Put it in the front.'

The excitement of leaving Darwin slowly fades like an unravelling jumper. Exhaustion washes over you, a left over from the adrenaline-fueled excitement you felt a few hours ago. As the car hums along, your eyelids droop. You sit up abruptly as the car slows, trying to grasp what's happening.

Danny motions with his chin toward a figure on the side of the road—a solitary person hitchhiking.

≠

The stranger leans on the bonnet, as if the effort required to hold up his substantial weight has become too much. 'Thanks for stopping fellas. I was dying out here.' A craggy, unshaven face stares at you from under the brim of an akubra. Sweat drips from his chin, making tiny pops as it hits the bitumen. Removing his hat he wiped his brow.

Danny leans across the passenger seat. 'Where are you going?'

'Home, Sydney,' the stranger says, face creasing into an ample smile.

Danny nods. You clamber out to let the man in. He swings his olive duffel bag off his shoulder and sticks out a meaty hand. It envelops yours but unlike Pug, he doesn't crush it. 'I'm Reg. Pleased to meet youse.'

You push the front seat forward. 'Sorry, it's a bit cramped in the back.'

'No problem. Better than standing in this bloody heat. Where can I stow my gear?'

Danny chimes up. 'Stick it next to you. We'll sort it out later.'

Relieved, Reg sinks into the seat with a sigh. 'Thanks again fellas. Jeez, I could murder a cold one.'

Smiling, Danny pulls back onto the highway. The open windows help remove the odour of sweat that's arrived in the car. You turn around to face Reg, keen to know more about him. 'How'd you end up hitchhiking all the way out here?'

Grunting, as if the memory is not a pleasant one, then with a sniff, 'I was at the rodeo and the blokes with me got fed up with the heat. They decided to leave, bloody city slickers. I stayed. You fellas on holiday?'

Danny nods. 'We're visiting my sister in Sydney.'

A booming laugh from Reg. 'A couple of country boys off to the big smoke.' He snorts, amused by his own humour. 'If youse don't mind, I'm gonna get some shut-eye. That heat took it outta me.'

It's not long before there's a rumbling from the back seat. Looking across at Danny, 'You gonna take him all the way to Sydney?'

He shakes his head. 'I dunno. We can, if he doesn't mind helping out.'

Reg's sleepy voice mutters, as much to himself as to Danny, 'I'm happy to help if youse want.'

Laughing, you look over your shoulder. 'Thought you were asleep.' He smiles, his eyes remain closed. Turning back to Danny, 'So where are we gonna stop and sleep tonight?'

Reg snorts. 'Under the stars, son. Lots of places to lie down. It's a big country.' He begins humming softly to himself.

You begin to understand why Reg may have ended up on his own. 'Reg, we don't have sleeping bags.'

He snickers as if it's a joke. 'We'll work it out. Shit I'm buggered.' He shifts position, the seat groans in protest, and five minutes later loud snoring fills the car. The trip has become far more interesting.

The glow from the Three Ways Roadhouse is a welcome sight as Reg, now wide awake, advises Danny not to drive too much further at dusk. 'Too many roos on the road. Big buggers too.'

'Should we get a cabin?' Danny and Reg both shake their heads as your sullen eyes watch Three Ways disappear.

'We should stop here. It's the best spot we've seen,' Reg exclaims, nodding enthusiastically at a truck lay-by. 'We can make a fire. That'll keep those nosey critters at a distance,' he adds, with a mischievous grin. You're curious about the critters he mentions, but you decide not to ask, knowing by now that Reg has a way of telling stories in his own time.

With a cheerful whistle, Reg heads off to gather firewood and returns with an armful of twigs and branches. 'This'll get us started.' As he strips off his shirt, his tanned, weathered skin contrasts vividly against the red, peeling on his shoulders. As the fire comes to life, casting a warm, flickering glow, you move to stand beside him, mesmerized by the embers in the darkening sky.

'That's impressive, Reg.'

Reg chuckles and shakes the box of matches in his hand. 'Gotta have a Redhead,' a twinkle in his eye. Unrolling his sleeping bag, he settles down, and snoring soon vibrates in the night air.

You toss and turn at the noise from passing road trains, their heavy engines thumping, as they rumble past. And in the far-off distance, the haunting yips of dingoes, Reg's critters you think. If you knew the importance of the day's events, you might not have been able to close your eyes at all.

The sign reads 'ELCOME TO EENSLAND' Bullet holes have obliterated the 'W'. Whoever did the shooting was either good or up close, likely the latter. The 'Q' and 'U' are gone too. A shit-encrusted cattle grid is the only other clue that you're entering Queensland. Disappointed, you turn to Reg. 'How much further?'

Reg laughs. 'We're not near Sydney. A way to go yet. You fellas should remember this spot, no idea when you'll be back.' There's a wistful note in his voice as he scans the horizon. 'Youse should take a picture.'

With a shake of his head, Danny is vehement. 'We gotta keep going or ...'

Reg interrupts. 'C'mon, it'll only take a few minutes.' With a miserable look, he reluctantly agrees.

Reg, holding his belly in mirth, takes immense pleasure in capturing a photograph of a pissed-off Danny and you, pushing the Volkswagen across the border with hands on its rear. He urges for more photos, adding to Danny's already sour mood. Little do you realise that the journey is about to descend into chaos as Reg casually mentions a spot at Isa that he wants to show you both. You feel that he's deliberately provoking him.

Gritting his teeth, Danny snaps in frustration, 'Fuck. We'll never get to Sydney at this rate.'

Nonchalantly, Reg mutters, 'Sydney's not going anywhere.'

The silence is worse than the griping, and you wait for an inevitable explosion. In Mt Isa, Reg directs Danny to a lookout, and you get a view of the town spread before you, dominated by tall smokestacks. The faint sounds of a working mine clunking and grinding in the distance. The town appears worn and withered, like a shredded coconut husk. Reg recounts stories of past conflicts between miners and the government.

'It led to people leaving. But she'll come back. She's a tough town.' With his hands in his pockets, Danny remains silent, a pained expression on his face.

You wander to a post with signs pointing towards cities worldwide: Cape Town, London, and Hong

Kong. Even the equator has a sign, not that it's a city. But the one that catches your attention sends a shiver up your back. The sign pointing to Sydney reads sixteen hundred miles.

'Shit,' you exclaim, 'Sydney's so far.'

His frustration resurfacing, Danny snaps, 'That's why we gotta keep moving.'

Reg, ever the optimist, tilts his head and winks. 'We'll be in Longreach tonight, then it's just a hop, skip, and jump to Sydney.' Chuckling at his remark, he returns to the car, seemingly unfazed.

As the miles of red, dusty plains pass, Danny's mood softens, and a smile creeps onto his face. But Reg has another suggestion. You suspect one he's been angling for all along.

'How about we stop and sample some of the local brew?'

Danny shakes his head. 'We must keep going.'

In a low voice, Reg says, 'You're on holiday. Relax.'

The tension between them rises, and you try to ease it, and take Reg's mind off a cold beer, if that's possible. 'Reg, why did you leave this place if you like it so much?'

The question hangs in the air, and Reg's jovial smile fades momentarily, replaced by a sombre expression. He looks out at the desolate landscape; his eyes fill with nostalgia and sadness. Appearing deep in thought, then he stirs. 'I dunno. Being in the bush makes me happy. I spent years out here as a ringer when I was about your age, Graham, maybe a bit older.' He pauses, 'Real friendly people, hardworking, decent folk. Do anything for you if you're genuine. They don't suffer fools.' He stops, lost in his memories, remaining silent.

You want to leave him alone but can't resist one more question. 'What's a ringer?'

Chuckling, 'They muster cattle Graham. The big properties have thousands of cattle. I loved being out in the bush in the early mornings when a silvery mist lay over the country as far as the eye can see. Then, as the sun rises, the day turns to a cloudless blue sky, and she gets hot. I got no truck with religion, but you gotta believe in something bigger than yourself when you're out here with no-one else for miles around. And at night the stars in an inky black sky are something special. Even puts the morning's cold beer to shame.'

Smiling, 'You a bit of a poet, are you, huh?'

'Nah. A simple bushy.'

You persist. 'Why aren't you still out here working then, as a ringer?'

Reg sighs. 'It's hard yakka.' Laughing, 'Anyway, I got me dream job. Working in a brewery.' He licks his lips and swallows. 'Speaking of which.'

You ignore the last part, knowing Danny is not going to stop. 'What did you eat out here?'

Reg grins. 'Whatever I could shoot. Plenty on the hoof out here.'

You consider what might be edible. Not much comes to mind. 'Rabbits?'

A choking sound from Reg. 'Rabbits! You can't eat them. They're crook. Roos you can but you gotta check for worms.' Now regretting that you asked, but Reg is on a roll. 'Of course, there's camel, if you can develop a taste for it. I couldn't. I like juicy steaks. The stuff you're used to, Graham.'

Outraged, you snap, 'I've eaten other stuff. I've eaten a snake.'

Reg holds up his hands. 'Whoa. I didn't mean anything.' Grinning, 'How did you end up eating a snake?' Annoyed, you remain silent. 'C'mon, tell us.' Danny concentrates on the road and doesn't join in the conversation.

Soothed, you continue: 'When I was young, we lived in Africa.'

Reg cackles. 'You're young now.'

Looking over your shoulder, you give him a hard look. He grins. 'I had it then. Me and a friend were camping. We wanted to cook mealy maize.'

Reg pipes up, 'That's not a snake.'

This time you give him a dirty look. 'You wanna hear or not?' He nods, a look of innocence crossing his face. 'We needed Carnation milk for the maize. To get to the closest shop we had to walk along a dirt track that ran past a chicken coop.' You pause, remembering how close you came to being bitten. 'Anyway, we're walking back and there's rustling in the grass near the coop. A snake darts through a gap in the wire fence, but a rock dislodges and it gets trapped, stopping an inch from my ankle. My friend had a machete and chopped its head off, we cooked it over a fire.'

Reg is quiet. 'Any idea what sort of snake? Was it poisonous?'

You shrug. 'No idea. My friend said with the head gone, it'd be okay.'

Reg leans forward. 'You like it?'

Shaking your head, 'I can't remember much, other than it was chewy.'

Settling back into his seat, 'Sorry Graham, shouldn't have doubted you.'

'I saw a black mamba too.'

Reg puffs. 'Is that a snake? You eat it?'

Laughing, 'Shit no, this was scary. We were going to a farm. My family and a Boer family, in his Land Rover. One of the boys wanted to stop for a piss. We pull up alongside a baobab tree and ...'

Reg interrupts. 'A what? Baybo ...?

'Baobab, there's lots of them in Africa. They look like trees that grow their roots at the top instead of in the ground. Anyway, as we stop, this snake rears up, standing higher than the top of the car. The man yells, "Close the windows," and we sped away. I tell you, that thing was scary.'

'But you didn't eat it?'

'Shut up Reg.'

A silence descends on the car as we pass through countryside dotted with silvery mallee trees and scrubby grass, bleak but beautiful in its own way. You begin to understand Reg's love of it. Reg, meanwhile, clears his throat as you pass through each town, making loud smacking noises with his lips, then staring mournfully out of the rear window as they disappear in a cloud of red dust. Soon, unable to hold his tongue any longer, 'If we can't stop for a drink, what about a shower and clean sheets?' Danny's lips form a thin line. 'Where are you thinking, Reg?'

'How about Brisbane? I've a friend there. Youse can go and check out Surfers for a coupla days. It's a good place to meet sheilas.' He laughs, thumping the back of your seat, sending you headfirst into the dash. 'Oops, sorry Graham,' patting you on the shoulder.

You rub your forehead, hoping it isn't split open. 'You got a girl, Reg?'

Shaking his head, 'Nah. But we're getting crabby cooped up in this tin can. It might do us all good.' He stared at the back of Danny's head.

Looking sideways at Danny. 'We could do with a break. What do you think?' Surprisingly, he nods in agreement, without any argument, even though he's spent the entire trip rushing to get to Sydney. *What's on his mind?* You find out soon enough.

≠

Close to Brisbane, Reg points to a group of shops off the highway. 'Drop me off here. Surfers is an hour further on.' Grabbing his bag, taking your elbow, he leads you away from the car. 'You won't leave without me, will you? I enjoy travelling with youse.'

'No. Of course not.'

'Okay. Get a motel, past Surfers, otherwise it'll cost you an arm and a leg.' He leaves with a slap on your back, a wink and a parting quip. 'Stay outta trouble and I'll see youse back here in three days?'

Danny gives a cursory wave before driving off. His reason for agreeing to stop soon becomes apparent. 'We should keep going. We don't need Reg. Sydney's not that far now.'

'That'd be a prick of a thing to do. He's a good bloke.' He holds his tongue, but you watch his jaw tighten. It isn't over, not yet.

As you cruise along the Esplanade at Surfers, the sun bathes everything in a warm glow, and the crash of waves fills the air. You admire the tanned girls in bikinis parading along the street, laughing and throwing coy smiles at the blonde surfers who are everywhere. Yet, a pang of self-consciousness washes over you. Compared to the beachgoers around you, you feel out of place in your western shirt and torn Amco jeans. Danny taps his fingers on the steering wheel, pulling the car over to stop near a motel by the beach.

You look up at the motel's facade and hesitate, recalling Reg's advice to find accommodation away from Surfers. In the back of your mind, you know you'd never fit in among the parade of tanned people.

'We should find somewhere out of Surfers.'

Danny yawns, then agrees. 'Okay.' He turns onto Cavill Avenue, and you leave Surfers behind as you search for a cheap motel.

≠

Reg's familiar face greets you with genuine happiness. Waving, he hurries over. 'Great to see you again. You had me worried.'

You'd considered telling him that Danny wanted to go on without him, but watching his joy, you suspect he probably knows. 'Did you have a nice time, Reg?' He nods as he wipes his brow with a handkerchief, struggling into the back seat. 'You putting on weight?'

Puffing, ignoring the jibe, 'It was fine. Tell me about youse. Did you see Surfers? Meet any sheilas?' You smile; Danny grimaces.

You want to share the details of your time, but Danny disagrees. 'We'll never hear the end of it,' he says.

A smile creeps across your face as you begin recounting the events, fully aware that once Reg knew, he'd never let you live it down.

By the time you finish telling the story, Reg is holding his belly, gurgling with delight, while Danny glares at you. Reg snorts, handkerchief in hand, wiping tears away. 'Let me get this straight.' He inhales, calming himself. 'You met two backpackers. That right?' His face goes a shade of blue as another fit of giggles takes hold. Taking another breath, regaining his composure, and in a solemn voice, as if explaining something of the utmost importance to a child, 'They like you, right?' You nod, enjoying this. Danny grips the steering wheel, his knuckles white, his face a blank mask. 'So, these girls become more interested in youse when they find out you're staying in a motel. That correct?' You don't answer, knowing there's more. 'Didn't I tell youse to be careful? These girls, they ask about the laundry and then disappear after they wash their clothes, correct?' The car fills with his belly laugh. You're concerned he might be having a heart attack as he presses his hands against his chest, roaring. 'And, and,' gasping, 'Youse wait in your room for them to finish.' Tears run down his cheeks as he splutters like a newborn baby.

'They said they wouldn't be long, Reg.' He's now having too much fun at your expense and you're beginning to regret telling him.

Danny turns to face you. 'I warned you.'

Reg ignores him. 'I suggested local sheilas, not backpackers. Gawd almighty. So now the cleanest backpackers in all of Australia are in Queensland, that's great.' He collapses into high-pitched giggles.

'Shut up Reg,' struggling to hold back a smile.

You cross the Queensland border into New South Wales, with no fanfare. You don't even see a sign. The landscape transforms into endless rows of green stalks. Reg explains, 'Sugar cane. It's a massive industry out here, but cutting it is ...' He's interrupted by the blaring sound of an air horn from a truck as it speeds past—the gust of wind from its passing rattles the car. Danny wrestles with the steering wheel to keep the car on the road.

Then, with a loud *CRACK*, the windshield explodes, splintering into a thousand pieces. You panic, grabbing the armrest.

'Fuck,' Danny shouts, as he struggles to maintain control. Reg's hand grips the back of your seat. Urging him to pull over, your heart pounds in your chest. Danny manages to bring the car to a stop, but his forehead sinks onto the steering wheel, moaning in disbelief.

You gaze at the gaping hole that once held a windshield. The remnants of shattered glass litter the car's interior. Running your trembling hands through your hair, you feel tiny glass fragments sprinkle into your lap. Relieved, when your hands come away unscathed, the absence of blood is a reassuring sign. Shocked, you shake your head, causing more shards of glass to tumble into your lap.

'You okay Reg? Danny?' Danny's face is ashen as he stares at the damage.

Reg taps you on the arm. 'C'mon. We can't sit here. Let's clean it up.'

'But it's smashed to pieces. Can we still get to Sydney?' Danny doesn't reply.

Reg walks around the car, inspecting it. 'What are you doing, Reg? It's the windscreen that got busted.'

He pats the roof. 'That was a hell of a rock. You never know if something else got damaged. Doesn't look like it though. Let's pull out the pieces. Be careful. Don't wanna cut yourself.'

Danny mumbles, 'Hope it doesn't rain.' As he finishes speaking, a rumble of thunder splits the early evening. Glancing skywards, you see dark clouds gathering in the distance.

Reg nods. 'Yeah, they get big storms in these parts. Better get moving.'

Exasperated, Danny mutters, 'It'll be slower now.'

The humidity-laden air is warm, but still, you shiver as it blows through the car. Pulling your shirt tight around your shoulders, you huddle below the dash to escape the wind. The noise hurts your ears. 'You okay back there Reg?' A muffled response. He's wrapped his coat around his head, like a Bedouin fighter.

Danny faces the worst of it—he has to withstand the wind in his face, his brow furrowed as he peers out of the window. Raindrops plop onto the bonnet. Your chest tightens. *Rain is all we need*. You glance at the ominous sky. Maybe there is worse to come.

Reg, above the din of the wind, shouts, 'There's a garage ahead. They might have something to cover it and stop this bloody wind.'

Danny nods and pulls in alongside a Golden Fleece pump, red with rust. 'You reckon that's working?'

Reg shrugs. 'We'll find out.' He clambers out. Stretching, he groans, 'Geez, I'll be glad when we arrive in Sydney,' as he disappears, you hear the door bang. Danny studies the darkening sky. The rain has held off, but he looks worried.

'You okay?'

'Some fucking holiday. This'll set me back a bit.' You want to cheer him up, telling him you'll help pay.

Reg returns, holding something aloft in his hand like a trophy. 'These places carry everything. I got this. The bloke said the town's not far from here. We should be able to get the screen replaced in the morning.' Reg begins whistling as he stretches the plastic screen across the window. You swear it's to annoy Danny. 'Now, if you trap the end of the plastic in the door when you close it, we'll be sweet.'

Danny mutters, 'Fuck, it's hard to see out of,' as he drives onto the highway. 'I'm as blind as a bat.' The wind noise is reduced, and you close your eyes, hoping the town isn't far. *BANG.*

The car shoots forward like a bullet from a gun, sliding across the road, tyres squealing as Danny hits the brakes to stop the car from going into a ditch at the edge of the road. Frightened, you look around, unsure of what has happened. Reg is swearing. Danny shouts, 'What the ...?'

Coming to a stop, the car is balanced precariously with one wheel in the ditch, there's a smell of hot oil. Your heart thuds, as memories of another accident surface. The sound of slamming doors, accompanied by angry voices coming from behind the car. Concerned that it might slip into the ditch, you get out with great care, the freed plastic screen flaps in the wind.

A stationary car sits in the centre of the road, headlights blazing, and four young men stand beside it. The boy near the driver's door moves towards you, a sneer on his face, his hands balled into fists. 'Why'd you pull out in front of us like that?'

Reg exhales. 'Hang on a minute, son. You hit us in the rear. We were in the middle of the bloody road.'

'You reckon?' he says, raising his hands. But then drops them, looking over his shoulder as blue flashing lights approach. Turning back, he snarls, 'You're fucking lucky.'

You don't know how the police got here so fast, but you're glad they did. The boy walks away as the police car comes to a halt and an officer struggles out, pulling his belt up over a large beer belly. Straightening his jacket, he marches towards the cars. 'What's happened here? Anyone hurt?'

The boy, now with his hands in his pockets, says, 'They caused it.'

The officer glares at him and repeats his question. 'Is anyone hurt?' The four boys shake their heads. We do the same. 'All right, what happened?'

The boy mutters sullenly, 'They pulled out in front of us. I couldn't miss 'em.' The officer gives him another hard stare. 'You're Charlie Pearson's boy, Ed, ain't you?'

A wicked smile appears on the boy's face. 'Yeah. Look, it's their fault.' The officer unclips a torch and shines it towards the boy's car. There's a dent in the centre of the chrome bumper. He shuffles across to the Volkswagen and spends a few minutes examining the rear, where there are large dents in both the bumper and boot, and then he shines the torch into the interior.

'They hit us squarely in the rear,' Reg says.

'You the driver?' Reg shakes his head, nods towards Danny. 'Alright. I'd like a word over here if you don't mind. Ed, you and your friends, be quiet and get out of the middle of the bloody road.'

Reg whispers, 'I got a bad feeling about this. We've got trouble.'

The officer returns, still struggling with his belt, his belly winning the battle. Danny trails behind him, looking like he's eaten a bad prawn. The officer, hands on hips, surveys the four boys and then us. 'I'm sure you can't go much further tonight. I'll arrange for your car to be towed to the local garage. Meanwhile, I reckon we can offer you some country hospitality.'

'What about the damage? Who'll pay?' Danny asks, motioning to the boys.

'I'll look into it. They say you pulled out in front of them. That piece of plastic would have made your vision difficult.' He turns to the four. 'Ed, your car able to be driven?'

Ed looks despondent, clearly having hoped you'd be hauled off directly to whatever they consider a jail around here. Dragging the toe of one shoe on the road, 'I guess.'

Still talking to the boys, the officer adds, 'I reckon you've all had enough for one night. Go home. I'll talk to your parent's tomorrow.' As a tow truck arrives, it crosses your mind that this may not have been the first accident to occur on this part of the highway.

Danny, eyes downcast, sits in the front of the police car. Reg, on the other hand, grins from ear to ear and licks his lips in anticipation when the officer says he'll arrange accommodation at the local pub.

You arrive to find the publican annoyed by his last-minute guests. 'Wadda you mean I'm putting them up for the night?' he asks, with a grim smile.

The officer snaps, 'It'll be taken care of.' The publican, with a defiant look on his face, wanders away, muttering about his good nature being taken advantage of—you haven't seen much of that nature yet.

Reg heads for the bar and sets up a beer for himself and Danny. 'Lemon squash for you, Graham?' You nod. Reg raises his glass. 'Don't be so down, fellas. We could have gotten hurt; instead, here we are having a beer.' He signals to the publican. 'I'll have another.' Dismayed, the publican moans loud enough for us to hear about being forced out onto the street if this keeps up. Reg downs his second beer in two gulps. 'Let's have dinner, get some sleep and, as they say in the classics, the rest will take care of itself.'

'I know what's going to happen. Nothing,' says Danny.

'You're right. I think the quicker we leave, the better. Those boys are locals and the copper knows their parents. Whatever we say won't matter.'

'I know, but that means we'll have to pay for the damage.'

'That's better than paying for both, and that could happen.'

≠

The officer made an early return. His uniform neatly pressed, sharp creases on both his pants and shirt, three stripes on the shirt sleeve.

'I've spoken to the mechanic,' he announces, his voice carrying a reassuring tone. 'He's already at work on your car, and you should be back on the road soon. The good news is that the motor's fine. He'll fit a new screen as well.'

Danny's jaw clenched as he once again voiced his concerns. 'What about the ones who hit us? Are they going to pay for the damage?'

The officer paused, drawing a deep breath, straightening himself, still a full head shorter than Danny. Meeting his gaze, the officer replied, 'Conflicting stories from both sides make it difficult to pinpoint blame. I believe it's best to call it even and move on. After all, we took care of you last night.'

Reg stepped in, aware of Danny's emotions, hoping to prevent any further heated exchanges. 'Thank you, officer. Your assistance is appreciated.'

The journey to the garage was tense. You glance across at Danny, a worried frown on his face, whereas Reg seemed content, wearing a satisfied expression, no doubt in memory of last night's beer. Meanwhile, you hope that you will still get to Sydney.

Reaching the garage, the officer signalled to the mechanic working on the car. The man peeked around the side. 'This is one tough beast,' he called out. 'Nothing wrong with the motor, just a bit of cosmetic damage. I've replaced the screen.'

Danny opened his mouth to say something. Reg, placing a hand on his arm, restrained him, and asked, 'How much?'

The mechanic scratched his ear, and stole a glance at the officer. Sensing the unspoken query, the officer inclined his head. 'A couple of hundred should sort it all out.' His eyes shifting between Reg and the officer.

As the officer walked back to lean against his car, keeping a watchful eye over the proceedings.

You move close to Reg, so you're not overheard. 'Can we do anything?'

Reg shakes his head. 'Those young fellas had a beer or two in 'em, is my guess. You look after locals, not strangers, in these towns. He's going to make damn sure they're okay.'

You can't help but wonder what other challenges lie ahead on this trip. You and Reg chip in to help pay for the repairs, but it does little to ease his mood. As you leave, the officer follows, 'like a good ol' western sheriff,' Reg mutters.

You relax, hoping all the problems are now behind you, the beginnings of a smile on your lips as you look forward to Sydney. You should've known better.

Part Two: Loss

Crossing Sydney Harbour Bridge, a sense of awe grows, as if a giant hand lifted the lid on a wondrous, magical jewelled box. The entire city unfolds before you, basking in sunlight and creating a dazzling spectacle as the windows of tall buildings glitter and reflect sunbeams in every direction. The harbour glistens in a shade of pea-green, with ferries gracefully gliding through the waters, their bows leaving behind a trail of white water. A single word comes to mind: Home.

Reg urges Danny to take the Cahill, emphasising his point by thumping the back of your seat. As you speed down the expressway, Danny maneuvers the car into the correct lane. You stare at an unusual structure covered in scaffolding; its shape resembles conch shells stuck together. It brings back a memory of searching for similar shaped shells on Hunstanton Beach. Curiosity gets the better of you. Over your shoulder. 'What are they building there, Reg?'

A glint of humour in Reg's eyes, 'That's gonna be an opera house, or at least it will be if they finish it.' He hesitates, then, with a shake of his head. 'It's a waste of money if you ask me.'

Suppressing a chuckle, 'No one did, Reg.'

His hand thumps your seat again, this time with force. He instructs Danny to turn at the next corner. He cuts across another lane, prompting a blast of horns from angry drivers. 'Follow this, then turn left at Pitt Street. I'll show you.'

As you venture further into the city, the sun disappears behind the towering buildings. Crowds of people hurry past, absorbed in their daily lives, barely sparing a glance at the sight of a red-dirt coated Volkswagen on their streets. Your anticipation grows the closer you get to the People's Palace.

Danny had stopped at a payphone to call his sister, on the way into Sydney. Watching him as he spoke into the mouthpiece, you see him tense and slam the handset into its cradle, then stride back to the car. You look at Reg, who, with a slight shake of his head, warns you to keep quiet. Danny says nothing as he gets back into the car. Then, strikes the dash, 'Bloody fuckin' hell. We have to change our plans.' Your heart drops as he continues: 'My sister's got a job and is staying at the YWCA in the city.'

'What? Why's that a problem?'

A guffaw from behind you. 'Can't stay there, it's only for girls. You won't even get through the front door.'

Danny's knuckles whiten as he grips the steering wheel. 'Thanks Reg, I know.'

'Can we stay with your aunt?'

Shaking his head, 'The rest of her family has turned up and she's got no fuckin' room. That's why my sister moved.'

Flinching away from the anger in his voice, 'Were on holiday. We'll be okay.'

Frowning, he moans, 'I'm nearly broke. The fuckin' car ...' raising his hand as if to strike the dash again, then thinking better of it. 'This is turning out to be a shitty holiday.'

'I know a place near the YWCA,' said Reg. 'Run by the Salvos, so it's pretty cheap. Umm, it's ... oh yeah, the People's Palace. A bit dodgy.' The implication hung in the air.

Blushing, 'I can take care of myself.'

Reg nodded. 'Sure, sure you can.'

Turning to Danny. 'Let's check it out. No harm staying a night or two.'

≠

It seemed like a reasonable thing to say at the time, but now, as you sit in the car outside a dishevelled old building, doubt creeps into your mind. *Is that it?*

Danny's face mirrors your uncertainty. He voices the nagging doubt. 'You sure it's got accommodation, Reg? Don't look like a palace.'

A weary smile on Reg's lips, 'No, a Palace it ain't, but it's better than the one over there.' He gestures towards a building across the street, its faded neon sign blinking *Rooms to let* above a grim entrance. The sight of a solitary figure, wrapped in a drab grey overcoat, rocking back and forth on the steps adds to its picture of misery. Passers-by choose to avert their gaze, shutting out the reality of his existence. 'That one's cheaper. But I wouldn't recommend it.'

You couldn't help but glance toward the alternative. Shivering, the mere thought of spending a night in that place sent a chill through you. Turning your attention back to the People's Palace, its worn and tired exterior also did little to inspire confidence.

Danny muttered, 'This one doesn't look much better.'

Reg laughs, poking him in the shoulder. 'Go round the corner, Campbell Street. That'll do me.' He gets out, inhales and shakes his head. 'I miss this place when I'm away.' Turning to you and Danny, 'Appreciate the lift, fellas.' He looks you in the eye. 'If you need me, I'll be at the Bellevue pub. Come say g'day. It's near Redfern station. Remember that, Graham. Bellevue.' 'Um, okay,' even though you don't expect to see him again.

He laughs. 'Make sure you do.' Hefting his duffel bag onto his shoulder, he waves, then walks off along Campbell Street, sweat-stained akubra perched at an angle on his head. You watch him go with a pang of loss. Then, with a shrug, anxious to start your holiday in Sydney, 'C'mon, let's go check out this place and catch up with your sister.'

Danny nods. 'I guess. Let's see what it's like inside.' He paces ahead, turning into Pitt Street. The man on the steps continues to rock on his heels, people still take no notice.

Pitt Street is different from the picturesque images of Sydney in your mind. It feels neglected, a stark contrast to the vibrant parts of the city you glimpsed on your way here. The People's Palace itself wears the weight of time. You imagined it once was grand but now it is a shadow of its former self. Standing before it, you can't help but wonder if it's even worth going inside. The adjacent cafe, bearing the same name, offers little reassurance with its unremarkable appearance. As if to confirm Pitt Street's descent into neglect, the nearby Paradiso Cafe is boarded up and forgotten.

You muster the courage to glance at your reflection in the window and recoil in horror. You see a boy with windblown hair and a faded western shirt hanging over torn jeans. You hastily tuck in the shirt, attempting to regain some semblance of neatness, but the jeans are beyond repair. There's one silver lining, at least you haven't yet begun shaving, unlike Danny, who now sports a wild beard.

Ascending the grimy steps into the foyer, your desert boots scuffing on the faded tiles, the sound of voices and clinking cutlery drift from the café's open door. The lobby's centre holds a glass-fronted booth that reminds you of a ticket box at a circus, but nothing is amusing about the figure within. It's the largest woman you've ever seen. As you approach, her expression reflects a mix of disdain and suspicion, as though she's sniffing the air for something offensive. Close-set eyes scrutinise you with distrust, beads of sweat glisten between the rolls of fat that form her chins. She raises a hand, adjusting her bun, and you can't help but feel a pang of discomfort under her scrutiny. It's as if she's judging you, making you aware that you don't belong here—another sniff, this one more pronounced, as if something terrible has assaulted her senses.

Danny smiles. 'We'd like a room. Please.'

With a cold laugh, nostrils flaring, 'For how long?'

'Uh, tonight ...'

'One night.' She cackles, bringing to mind witches and boiling black pots. 'This isn't a doss house. There's a minimum three-night stay. And no shared rooms.' She turns away and picks up a book, placing tortoise-shell glasses on her nose, ignoring us. Turning a page, concentrating on the words.

Stammering, you ask, 'How, how much for ... for four nights?'

There's a pause as she runs her finger along the edge of a page, bending a corner to mark her place, and closing the book with a snap, followed by an exaggerated sigh. 'A hundred dollars for four nights. Includes towel and soap.' As she places the book on the counter, you sneak a look at the cover, 'Portnoy's Complaint'. It means nothing to you, but she notices and bristles, her upper lip twitching as she slides the book off the counter. 'Do you want the rooms or not?'

'Um, uh, yes, we do. We will,' Danny says.

'There's one on the first floor, the other is on the third. You're not allowed on the women's or family floors. There's a television room on the third floor. No television after nine.' She announces this in a voice reminiscent of a school principal, then places two pieces of paper and a pen in a tray at the bottom of the glass. 'Fill these out.'

The room is tiny, cramped, and barely big enough to stretch your arms without brushing against each wall. The worn, cracked linoleum floor beneath your feet speaks of years of use. The room houses two pieces of furniture:

a weathered, one-door cupboard and a solitary iron bed with a towel and a bar of Palmolive soap placed on it.

The bed creaks and groans under the weight of your body as you lie down. The mattress sinks. Hands cradling the back of your head, you let out a contented sigh. You can't believe it. *I'm in Sydney.*

≠

Pacing up and down in front of the YWCA, your heart beats faster. Anticipation bubbles, and with each step, you feel a mix of excitement and anxiety. Puffing out your chest, you feel good wearing your latest possession—a buckskin vest, grateful that it masks some of the wear and tear of your tattered shirt. Still, it can't hide every imperfection, the frayed collar and sleeves.

You recall the salesman's face when you said you'd wear it out of the shop.

'Excuse me sir, you don't want it in a bag, is that correct, sir?'

'I'm gonna wear it now.

'An expression of horror crosses his face, his hands flutter, the sophisticated attitude vanishes. With an effort he regathered himself. 'Uh, oh, very well. Should I leave the price tag on sir?' You miss the sarcasm. He rummages in a drawer, pulling out a pair of pink-handled scissors.

Muttering, he cuts off the tag, handing you a bag with 'Farmers' on it. 'Just in case, sir,' he says, turning his back.

Your eyes search the surroundings, hoping for a glimpse of her. The woman inside glares, her manner unwelcoming. Moving out of her sight, worry gnaws in your chest. *Where is she?*

The weight of the buckskin makes you feel like nothing can penetrate it or you. Glancing in the window, yes, well worth the thirty-five dollars. You turn your mind back to Danny's sister. *How do you tell her he's not coming, that you had a fight? Will she blame me?* Smacking your hand against your thigh. *Damn it.*

#

The first meeting with Lisa did not go as expected. She was waiting, arms folded across her chest, on the steps of the YWCA. If Danny expected a warm welcome, he was disappointed. She rolls her eyes. 'You two could do with a shower.' A wisp of auburn hair across her face; a flick of her fingers and it was gone. She continued, 'Hmm. I can't invite you in, you know.'

Danny, in an icy tone, 'Nice to see you too, sis.' Your heart pounds as you look at her brown eyes, with tiny specks of green floating in them.

Raising her hand, she barks, 'I'm tired, I've gotta work early. But you can come back tomorrow night and we'll go for drinks. Some friends of mine will be there, so be nice brother.' She studies you, the faint beginnings of a blush on your face. 'Are you old enough to get into a pub?'

Lowering your eyes as if you were back in school. 'Yes, I am, I mean ...'

'Okay. See you at seven. And clean yourselves up.' Spinning on her heel, she walks back inside. Danny, red-faced and irritated, trudged back to the Palace.

'Is she always like that?'

'Yeah. We don't get on.'

'No kidding.'

'I thought she might've changed. It seems not. Fuck her. To hell with it.'

'You've come all this way. It'll be better tomorrow.'

A knot of regret twists in your stomach, you should've bitten your tongue. The night hadn't gone well. Danny and Lisa didn't speak to each other. He scowled at her friends. Whenever the conversation drifted to the trip, his responses were sharp and dismissive, effectively shutting down any chance of pleasant conversation. Lisa pouted, and ignored us until we left. Then, surprisingly, invited us to a party, her parting remark, aimed at her brother, held a hint of frustration, 'It'll be fun. Might help if you're more pleasant, brother.'

The next day, on your way back from Danny's aunt's place, you try to persuade him to attend the party. Looking over your shoulder, at the lemon meringue pie melting into a white goo. You turn back to Danny, determined, 'We promised we'd go.'

His eyes remain fixed ahead, lips drawn into a thin line, his emotions smouldering beneath the surface. 'I don't care. We should leave. I've had enough.'

Unsure of what he means. 'Leave? And go where?'

'She's not interested. She only cares about her stuck-up friends,' he replied bitterly.

Trying to sway him, 'We still have two nights left at the palace and the party's tonight. C'mon, let's go.'

Danny took a deep breath. 'I've had enough. I want to leave.'

His words stung, but a part of you had expected this. 'Enough of what? We've only been here a few days. Is this just about your sister?'

His frustration boiled over, as he pounds the steering wheel with a clenched fist. 'Fuck her. She doesn't care. I say we leave and I'm driving, so I decide.'

'Well I want to stay.'

His eyes bulge, and his face twists in rage as he shouts, 'I don't care. I need your money to get home. So, we're doing what I say.'

In anger, you dig into your pocket pulling out a handful of notes, throwing them at him. 'Then go. If it's only money you want, take it.'

He snatches up the money, as you slam the door and storm back to the palace. Back in your room, you count out what's left. *Shit, one hundred and sixty-five dollars. Fuck. Fuck. FUCK!*

≠

'Where is he?' Her voice catches you by surprise. Turning, your mouth drops open. A silk top proudly displays her full breasts. Her eyes watch yours, your face heats up.

'He's your brother. You know how he is.'

She wipes a hand across her brow, as if swatting away an annoying fly. 'His loss. It'll be fun tonight.'

'Why? What's happening?'

She winks. 'Wait and find out. Is that a new jacket?'

'Yeah, great, isn't it?'

'If you say so. C'mon, let's go. We gotta get a cab. The party's in Bondi.'

You caress the fabric, feeling its weight, disappointed by her remark. *What's wrong with it?*

Lisa hails a cab and directs the driver, settling gracefully into her seat. You like being in her company, thankful now that Danny isn't here. You try to control the longing in your heart, clasping your hands tightly against your thighs resisting the desire to touch her. A smile escapes your lips, content to sit alongside with your dreams.

As she gazes out of the window, she's unaware of the fire burning inside you, the driver also follows her every move through the rear-view mirror. Lisa remains oblivious to his attention too. The cab halts in front of a towering high-rise building, and as you step out onto the glistening streets, still damp from recent rain, you pull your vest close to shield yourself from the chilly wind.

The distant sound of waves crashing on a nearby beach evokes the reminder of Fannie Bay Beach. You suppress a shiver, not caused by the cold breeze but rather by the urge to suggest a stroll along the beach, hand in hand like lovers. But you quickly dismiss the thought.

Lisa grabs your shoulder. 'They live on the top floor. C'mon.'

She pushes the button marked 18, the lift rises quickly, gliding to a silent halt. As the doors open, she hurries to the door opposite and bangs on it with her palm. The song 'My Girl' blasts out as the door opens, accompanied by a heady smell you instantly recognise. A bare-chested man stands in the doorway, long dreadlocks, white and yellow sarong around his waist. His ebony body shines with sweat and his face cracks into a beaming smile. 'Hey, you made it, crazy,' pulling her into his chest. She wraps her arms around him, they kiss, your heart hits the bottom of your feet. Holding his hand, she introduces him as Samuel, smiling in a way you haven't seen her do in the short time you've known her. You're no longer looking forward to the remainder of the night.

The room he ushers you into is small. Ten people sit in a circle, cross-legged on the floor. A man in a beaded kaftan is singing along to 'My Girl' in a rich baritone voice. A girl moves over to make room for you as Lisa sits next to Samuel, who wraps a protective arm around her. You stare glumly at the carpet.

'Man, have I got a surprise for ya all.' Samuel laughs. 'Now my Lisa is here.' Standing up, opening a cupboard, a feeling of expectation rises around the circle. The shelves are empty apart from one, in the centre a square block no larger than a sugar cube, wrapped in foil. Lisa squeals. A smattering of hands clapping. 'This is the best hash you'll get anywhere, man,' Samuel says, 'I bring it in myself,' picking it up between his finger and thumb. His next words chill you to the bone. 'Hope everyone here can handle strong shit.' This could be your worst nightmare.

Samuel unwraps the block as the girl beside you magically provides a double-edged razor blade and begins scraping slivers of hash onto the foil. Someone offers cigarette papers and a tin of tobacco. The girl takes a pinch of tobacco, lays it on the cigarette paper, and then sprinkles the hash over it. She rolls the joint, twisting and licking both ends, handing it to Samuel, who lights up. There's a hushed silence as everyone waits their turn. He passes the joint; greedy fingers waving in the air, waiting for it. It reaches you. Quaking as if it's a stick of dynamite, you place it between your lips, inhaling, then sputtering and coughing. Samuel, a smug look on his face, 'Told you it was the best shit. Pass it on.'

Lisa leans forward, the silk top slipping down, off one of her ivory shoulders. 'You okay?'

Eyes fixed on her shoulder, you nod, unable to speak. More joints make their way around the circle. Your lips are numb, your head spins. Lisa's face swims into view, but not the Lisa you know. This one has blazing green eyes and a mouth crammed with rotting teeth.

A bang startles you. Someone yells, 'Fuck, it's the cops!'

Panicking, staggering to your feet, mumbling, 'Gotta get out.' Legs shaking like jelly, swaying back and forth. The balcony, go that way. Grabbing the curtain, your other hand searching for the door handle as you hear loud laughter behind you.

'Stop, stop, it's a joke,' Samuel cackles. 'Sit down.' He's rolling on the floor holding his stomach. Blinking, you look at him, dazed, confused, your grip on the curtain tightening. Samuel wheezes, eyes lit up. 'Were you gonna jump?' His belly shakes again. Stumbling back to the circle, flopping to the floor, you cover your head in your hands.

Lisa prods you with her foot. 'Are you alright? You don't look good.'

'Uh, I'm, mmm ... need, need to ...' with trembling legs, you force yourself to rise again. The bathroom is a few steps away but appears much further. You pray it's unoccupied, pushing the door open, collapsing onto the cold, black-and-white tiles, nausea twist your insides. The toilet is in front of you, yet each movement feels like an eternity.

Your stomach can't hold back any longer. Yellow and green bile erupts from your mouth, spraying across the floor. Moaning, hands coated in the slime, head pounding like a drum, you crawl towards the toilet bowl. Resting your cheek against the cool porcelain, you whimper, *please let me die.*

Time loses its meaning as you cling to the toilet bowl. Your stomach is empty, yet the agony persists. Summoning the last ounce of strength, you drag yourself to the sink, spitting out the lingering remnants. A hollow feeling grips you as you watch it spiral down the drain. The embarrassment and fear of becoming a laughing stock taunts you. And then there's Lisa— her image hovers in your mind, adding to your pain. *What will she think?*

The reflection in the mirror is of a white face with red-rimmed eyes. Seeing the floor awash with vomit, you drop back down to your hands and knees, and using toilet paper, begin to mop up the mess, pausing frequently to dry-heave, your throat raw and aching. Each movement is another stab in your stomach.

Once you've finished cleaning, you totter to the door, opening it slightly to peer into the lounge room. The air is heavy with smoke from incense sticks and hash. One person is asleep, curled up on the floor, but no sign of Lisa or Samuel. The thought of facing them fills you with dread.

Carefully stepping around the sleeping figure, you lie down. You're jolted awake by loud voices nearby. Squeezing your eyes shut, feigning sleep, praying for it all to end. *What could I say anyway?* A perfume you recognise wafts through the room. A skirt rustles, a heel clicking on the kitchen tiles.

'At least he cleaned up, not like the other one,' Lisa says, stepping over you. A door bangs. *How can I ever tell her?* You fall into a troubled sleep, dreaming of Lisa's green speckled eyes and a smile that grips your heart. The rest is a blur, involving a black man with braided hair.

Bright sunlight pierces your eyelids like a thousand needles, bringing an end to the dream. Raising your head off the carpet, the stink of vomit and hash in the flat is overwhelming. You had to get back to the Palace. *Danny will wonder where I am.*

As you wait for a bus, you sniff your clothes, your nose wrinkles in distaste. Your mouth is furry. The motion of the bus lulls you back into a fitful sleep, until its squealing brakes wake you. Apologising to the driver as you stumble down the steps. Your worst nightmare unfolds: she's in the booth, sneering, watching you shuffle across the foyer, taking note of each step. You let out a huge breath when she looks away.

Clutching the handrail, struggling up the stairs to Danny's room. Each step is a burden as your heart races and your mind rehearses the words you hope will make things right with him. Summoning your last energy reserves, you knock on his door, desperately waiting for a response that doesn't come. Leaning against the door, you give in to exhaustion, it swings open and sends you stumbling into the room, landing flat on your face, gasping for breath.

As you lie there, trying to regain your composure, your eyes focus, but what you see shocks you. The room is empty. A guttural moan escapes from the depths of your being.

Stumbling back to your room, irritation and frustration consume you as you're unable to find the key, and panic begins to set in at the thought of having to ask HER for another key. *Where is it? How could I have lost it?* You delve into your pocket once again with shaking hands. You feel the cold metal shaft, your fingers slide against each other, slick with sweat. Relief washes over you, but it's short-lived as the key slips through your trembling fingers, and clatters across the floor. *Shit. No.* You scramble on hands and knees, desperately searching for it. Drained, you only want to collapse into bed. Crying out in frustration you pound your fists against the door. From the adjacent room, you hear faint grumbling and shuffling, causing you to halt and listen anxiously. The noises subside. You spot a glint of metal from the corner of your eye. Grabbing the key, hurriedly inserting it into the lock and turning, but it resists. Desperate, you try again, tears welling in your eyes. Finally, with a savage twist, the key turns with a satisfying *clunk*. Pushing the door open, you collapse into your room and let the door shut behind you.

≠

Butter drips from the burnt toast, as if mocking you as your stomach rolls at the thought of eating it. You pick at the edge, until, in disgust, shove the plate out of sight. Looking around the cafe, there's an old man seated in the far corner, face waxen, a brown cardigan wrapped around his chest like a bandage. With a shaky hand he picks up his cup, the contents slosh over the lip into the saucer. With an effort, you can hear across the room, he raises the cup to his lips; then slurps. Wheezing, lowering the cup, managing to get it back on the saucer with a rattle. You wait for him to repeat the process, but he appears to have drifted off to sleep. You sneak a look at the only other person in the café, the buxom lady behind the counter. When you ordered toast with a Coke, her *humph* suggested it was not an ideal breakfast.

Turning away you stare out the window at the people passing by on Pitt Street, the wind forcing them to hunker down in their coats, umbrellas appear as the rain starts again. With a sigh, considering if you should go and find Lisa, tell her about Danny and explain last night. Your lips pressed together—bad idea, anyway you have no way to contact her. *Can't hang around outside the YWCA hoping I'll bump into her. Face it, I'm on my own.* Returning to Darwin goes through your mind. *No, not yet.*

A noise on the stairs gets your attention. A boy about your age wearing a red top hat, mop of blonde hair underneath is scolded by an old lady waving an umbrella. He ignores her and strides across the foyer, giving the impression that he owns the world.

Your spirits lift, you want to meet him.

Frantically, you peer through the window, trying to spot where he goes. But he vanishes from sight, leaving you longing to catch up with him. The rain is heavier, beating on the pavement in a steady tattoo as you hasten outside, not sure what you'll say if you do find him, but knowing you must try. Scanning the street in both directions, he seems to have vanished into thin air. *Where the fuck did he go?*

Suddenly, a flash of red catches your eye. You dash towards it, rehearsing words, eager to introduce yourself. But your excitement dies when you realise it's an elderly lady wearing a red scarf. You apologise and move on, feeling deflated. *He can't just disappear, can he?*

Undeterred, you search the nearby laneway, full of scattered wooden crates and a mattress leaning against a padlocked door. You're almost sure he's not here. With each passing moment, the initial thrill starts to fade. Seeking shelter from the wind and rain, you huddle in a doorway, feeling disheartened. *There must be a way to find him.* The idea of asking the Bun his room number crosses your mind, but you dismiss it. *No. She won't help.*

As you brace yourself to venture back out into the storm, a handwritten note taped on the window catches your eye. It advertises three-course meals for five dollars. *Shit that's good. I've got to remember this place.* You make a mental note of where you are.

The wind howls, and you pull your collar up to shield yourself, as you return to the Palace, hoping to spot the boy in the red top hat again.

Back in your room, the weight of last night haunts you. Unable to bear it any longer, you head for the television room. Glad to be out of the confinement of your shoebox, you flop onto a couch. *What am I going to do?*

To your amazement, the boy in the red top hat enters the room. Water droplets cascade from the brim of his hat. Spying you, he stops and removes the top hat.

A smile crosses your face. 'That's a great hat.' It's all you can think to say.

He grins. 'Yeah. I bought it at the cross. I get strange looks, but what the fuck. I'm Kevin,' he says, sitting next to you. The words tumble from you in an unstoppable flow, as if you've been friends forever. You tell him about Darwin, the trip and, with a tremor in your voice, Danny leaving. 'What'll you do?'

Shrugging, you don't reply. *What will I do?* Looking out the window, blue sky appears through the clouds, the rain gone, but it doesn't cheer you up. Kevin talks about his own family, then pauses, lowering his eyes, a dark patch forms on the lounge as tears drip from his chin. Both of you are silent, lost in your own thoughts.

A man enters and shuffles past, a blue raincoat over his shoulder. With a grunt, he takes a seat in a vinyl chair opposite, and begins drumming his fingers on one arm. His skin is the colour of dried porridge. He glances across, eyes stopping on you and then on Kevin. Ignoring him, you turn to Kevin. 'I found a place where for five bucks you get a three-course meal. I'm gonna go tonight. You wanna come?'

Kevin nods. 'Yeah. That sounds good.'

The man speaks, his voice reminds you of dull razor blades scraping on metal. 'There's plenty of those joints here.' He sucks in air, snuffling, then continues, 'If you need a quid, might be able to help youse out.' Squinting at him, not sure you heard correctly. A blank expression on his face, as he wipes his hands on the raincoat. 'There's a place over there.' He lifts his chin, indicating across the road. 'They got an office window that's always open. A person ...' looking at you, 'Mebee your size could squeeze through. Might be a few quid in there for youse.'

Kevin mutters, 'No fuckin' way.'

The man leans forward, grins and then stands. At the door he stops, pulls the raincoat around his shoulders. Looking back, his eyes shift from you to Kevin. 'It's there if youse want, let me know.' He leaves, along with an aroma of rotting vegetables.

Five dollars buys three slices of roast beef, potato, pumpkin and buttered bread—only two slices, the man behind the bain-marie says, shaking his finger—a cup of tea and a bowl of vanilla ice cream.

Kevin, mouth full of meat and gravy, mumbles, 'Eat up. Never ...' He burps. 'Never know when you'll have your next meal.' Stuffing more food into his mouth, as if he's late for an appointment.

He explains, about his father, how he died in a work accident. Taking a deep breath, he mentions his step-dad. 'When mum remarried, he didn't want me around. He'd hit me. Mum said nothing. He's a ....' He shakes his head as he mops up the last of his gravy with tiny pieces of bread that disappear into his mouth. Pausing, he eyes your plate, in his hand is the last piece of bread. Reaching across, he dips it into the gravy. 'Have you decided what you'll do?'

You have, but it sounds stupid every time you run it around in your head. Holding your breath, then exhaling, 'I wanna stay in Sydney. There's nothing for me in ...

in Darwin. But ...' Hesitating, remembering Craig's pleading eyes, and how you promised. 'I have a friend, umm, in Mount, uh, Mount Gambier. I was going with Danny, but now that he's ....' Voice trailed into silence.

'That's a long way from here. You're not gonna hitch, are you?'

'No. I'll catch the bus. I haven't got a lot of money left, but it shouldn't be too much.'

'When are you going?'

'Tomorrow. I'll look for a job when I get back.' You stare into the distance, knowing it all sounds fanciful.

He wipes his lips, slurps up the last of his tea. Putting the cup down, he looks thoughtful. 'C'mon, let me show you around. We can go to the snooker room. Gotta be careful though, it's a Sharpie hangout.'

'Sharpie? What's a Sharpie?'

He grins, looking at you as if you're from another world. 'Shit, where've you been?' You wait for him to continue. 'Sharpies think they own the streets.' He pauses. 'I guess they do. Some wear metal-capped boots and roam around in gangs, and like to kick the shit out of anyone they don't like.' He laughs, picking at his nose, inspecting it closely, then losing interest, flicks it on the floor. 'That's you and me, coz they hate long hairs. That's what they call us, long hairs,' he says, smiling. 'Anyway, stay away from em, if you see 'em.'

Kevin's eyes fix on every shop window you pass. A peculiar expression dances across his face. There's an air of mystery about him, a sense that some things are better left unquestioned when it comes to Kevin. Arriving at George Street, the bustling crowd push and shove you both as they hurry to wherever they're going.'

I want to show you something.'

Perhaps it's your full stomach that dulls your senses or that you're enjoying his company. 'Is it the Sharpie place?'

He shakes his head. 'Nah. That's over the road,' motioning to a building across the street. A lopsided dingy sign hangs above a set of dirt smeared steps. You make can out the word *Room*, but no *Snooker* anywhere on the sign. Chuckling, 'This is better. It's got whips and stuff.'

'What do you mean whips?' He doesn't respond, as he heads down a dimly lit laneway. You follow, the darkness engulfing, your palms clammy. Small shapes scurry across your boot, with a yell, you lash out, it squeals and darts away. Kevin stumbles, kicks a bottle against the wall, where it shatters.

A light above a doorway illuminates a man mountain who would not be out of place working as a lumberjack. Massive arms folded across his forty-plus chest, a bull neck bulging over his shirt collar. 'What the fuck are you kids doing here? Get lost or I'll smack you one.'

In horror, you watch Kevin flip two fingers in his direction. The man takes a step towards you. Kevin turns, races away, and you sprint after him, glancing back to make sure he isn't giving chase. Back on George Street, Kevin's bent double, wheezing. 'One day. I'll, I'll get in there,' he pants.

'What the fuck is that place?' He shakes his head, struggling to breathe. 'Are you okay?' His breathing slows and he nods. 'I got asthma. It's a fuckin' pain.'

His face is ghostly white. Holding onto your arm, the snooker room forgotten, you help him back to the Palace. On the steps, hesitating—the Bun is in the booth.

To delay the inevitable, you take Kevin aside to where she can't see you. Before saying goodbye, you ask about his plans while you visit your friend. Kevin's voice lowers, 'I'll go see me mum.'

Gripping his arm. 'You'll come back? Won't you? I don't, I haven't got...'

He smiles. 'Yeah. I'm gonna help you find a job.' He leans closer. 'Take your stuff. They'll let you leave it but they'll charge you.'

Nodding, wishing now you weren't going. You want to put an arm around him, but showing affection is not something you're used to. Instead, you punch him on the arm and promise to be back in a few days. As you stride past the Bun and up the stairs, her eyes follow.

Little did you know, had you stayed, you might have been able to alter the course of events.

≠

Settling into your seat on the Greyhound bus, memories of surprising Craig at his school in your mind. His delighted expression made you smile. The pretty red-headed girl, Regina, came to mind too, but it didn't go as expected. Craig warned you to stay away from her. Now, you're looking forward to reuniting with Kevin.

A man in a disheveled tie-dyed T-shirt and unkempt hair boards the bus, you tense, not sure why. Keeping a watchful eye on him as he passes and slumps into the seat behind you, humming to himself.

After a few hours on the road, the bus driver stops, for a half-hour break, he yells, climbing out of the bus. Your budget is stretched thin from the trip so you skip buying anything. Finding the restroom empty, leaning over the cold-water tap you take refreshing mouthfuls of water. The door opens, you recognise the humming.

Cautiously, raising your head, assessing the distance to the exit and calculating how quickly you could reach it if necessary. The man in the tie-dyed T-shirt greets you with a mumbled hello. Nervously wiping your mouth, you nod, stepping away from the sink, attempting to create a clear path to the door. He stands between you and the door, unaware of your unease. Instead, with a smile, he asks, 'Where are you headed?'

Eyes moving from his face to the door, 'To Sydney. Meeting a friend.' you want him to know someone's waiting for you.

He nods. 'Me too. Sydney that is.' Leaning on the washbasin, staring at his reflection in the mirror. It's hard to tell whether he likes what he sees. Brushing a hand through his hair, he turns and faces you. 'I hate to ask, but ...' He inhales. 'Could you lend me a ... a few dollars? I haven't eaten for a while.' His eyes are the colour of wheat, and there's a plea in them that touches the part of you that understands what it's like to be hungry. But you don't have much money left.

Counting in your head, 'I can give you five dollars.' That'll leave a hundred, a bed for four nights at the Palace, but no food.

His face lights up. 'That would be great.' Pulling a crumpled note from your pocket, holding it out towards him. He snatches it from your hand and scampers away without a backward glance. You smile at the sight of the five dollars clasped tightly in his hand. With a sigh, turning back to the tap; if you can't eat, water will have to do. As you bend over the tap, a cold shiver runs up your spine, as if someone walked over your grave, as your mother liked to say. You lift your head to see eyes, lacking any hope, stare back at you. Looking away, you turn off the tap, and pray Kevin will be waiting.

Arriving in Sydney, alighting from the bus, you hoist your bag onto your shoulder. Out of the corner of your eye you see the man in the tie-dyed T-shirt heading in your direction. Steeling yourself, determined not to give him any more money, you wait for the request.'

Thanks again for the money. I really appreciated your help. I'd like to repay it in some way.'

'Umm, there's no need.'

'Look, I don't live far from here. You're welcome to come along. You look like you could do with a hot meal. It's a shared house so lots of people drop by.'

What choice do I have? The money will only get you accommodation. *He seems harmless—murderers don't wear tie-dyed T-shirts, do they?* With a shrug, the thought of a hot meal won. 'Okay. For a little while. I need to … to sort out where I'm going to stay.' No need to tell him about the Palace.

With a cheerful expression, he sets off, and you follow, trying your best to memorise each turn as he leads you along narrow streets flanked by decaying terrace homes.

During the walk, he shares stories of his career as a dancer in stage shows. With a friendly pat on your shoulder and a smile, he exclaims, 'I'm pretty sure the hot meal will make you feel better.'

He stops before a wrought-iron gate, a single rusty bolt attached to a fence holds it in place. The paint has flaked away, revealing bare metal. The gate groans as he opens it and dashes up the steps, pausing to look back at you with a broad grin. 'I know it may not seem much. Come in.' He swings the door open, and laughter and music greet him. With your stomach in knots, you ascend the steps one by one, unsure of what to expect inside.

'Hey everybody, guess who's back?' he yells, disappearing inside.

You see a lot of people lying on the floor, others laughing and hugging or moving to the music, most in tie-dyed T-shirts like your friend, feather necklaces and bangles also appear to be a popular item. There's an unmistakable aroma of meat and other rich flavours in the air, and that now familiar earthy smell.

'Gordon, welcome back,' someone yells. 'How was the trip?'

He waves and grins. 'It was great.' Taking your arm, 'Grab a seat,' motioning to a bright-orange beanbag, a girl fast asleep in one alongside. 'I'll get you some food.'

He heads to the rear of the house batting away a chorus of questions. No-one takes any notice of you. When he returns, he's carrying a steaming plate. 'Here, dig in man.'

It's a curry, rich and exotic and you delight in every mouthful, scraping the last morsel off the plate. Looking around you decide it's time to go. Plate in hand, struggling up out of the beanbag, you go looking for Gordon. He isn't in the lounge room, but you do find him in the kitchen, his arms wrapped around another man. Halting, not sure what to do, you turn to go when he notices you, freeing himself from the man's embrace. 'Did you enjoy the curry?' nodding towards the empty plate. Brendan is the cook.

Embarrassed, you look down at your feet. 'Sorry, I didn't mean to ... I, I gotta go.'

'It's okay. Come, I'll walk out with you.'

Breathing in the fresh air, you relax, feeling bad about the way you reacted in the kitchen as Gordon takes hold of your wrist. 'Thanks again for helping me out. Here, I've got something for you.' He ferrets around in his jeans. 'I can't give you any money, but take these,' pressing something into your palm. You shake your head, protesting, but he says, 'It's okay, really.' Glancing down, you see the word *'HAIR'* in bold letters on the tickets. 'Take them. That's all I have.'

Stuffing them into your pocket, you turn to walk away, but Gordon pulls you back and wraps his arms around you in a tight embrace. Stiff as a board, your mind goes blank. No-one's hugged you like this before—not lovingly. He releases you, and steps back. 'Again, thanks for the help.' Your heart stops racing as you turn away to hide the tears that are trickling down your cheeks, and mumble a goodbye.

The bag over your shoulder weighs you down as you trudge towards the People's Palace, weary and exhausted. Thoughts of that embrace lingering—both comforting and unsettling. Shaking your head, you realise it's too difficult to understand the emotions it has stirred up. There are more pressing matters. Nonetheless, the tickets tucked safely in your pocket are evidence that the moment was real. You wonder what you'll do with them. *Maybe I can sell them?* Halting on the steps of the Palace, you sigh. *Doesn't she ever go home?*

The Bun rolls her eyes as you approach. 'You're back?'
'Yes, can I ...'
She interrupts. 'The Major wants to speak with you.'
'The Major? Who ... me? Why? Can I, why?'
'He said if you came back, you had to see him before you were allowed to have a room. That's why.'

'Tomorrow, I'm ...'

Slamming her hand down on the counter, 'If you want a room, you'll speak with him now.' She nods towards the office. Beads of sweat break out on your forehead as you approach the door. Looking over your shoulder, you see the Bun's eyes glint with satisfaction, like she knows what's about to happen.

You knock. A voice like a breeze through grass whispers, 'Come in.' A thin-faced man, a pair of rimless glasses perched on the end of his cherry-coloured nose, studies you as you enter. He nods towards a chair in front of his desk. You oblige, trying to figure out what's going on.

The man stands, slipping off his dark-blue jacket and hanging it on a coat rack that leans at an odd angle against a timber bookshelf. There's a single book on those shelves. His chair squeaks as he sits and fiddles with a peaked cap resting on a pile of papers, eventually glancing at you. *Why isn't he saying anything?* Nerves taut, you wait.

Removing his glasses, the man polishes them with a handkerchief, as the silence continues. Then: 'I'm Major Freck.'

You open your mouth. 'Uh, umm, the lady, she ...' Pointing back towards the door. 'She said you wanted to talk to me, if I ...?'

'Yes. Quite, quite,' he mutters. 'I'm concerned about ... about a friend of yours. Let me ...' He removes the cap from the pile of papers. Shuffling through them, he picks one up, squints at it over his glasses. 'Ah yes, Kevin Watts, that's his name. He's your friend?'

Why is he asking about Kevin? And is it the same Kevin? 'Um, I don't know his surname.'

The sheet of paper goes back down on his desk. Removing the glasses once again, rubbing his eyes, staring at you, 'Let me get this right. He's the boy that wears that silly hat, correct?'

'Oh, yes. He's my friend.'

Shaking his head, 'Your friend has caused a lot of trouble for one of our elderly residents.'

You hesitate, not completely surprised. 'He wouldn't.' *What has he done now?* A lump grows in the pit of your stomach as you wait. *What's happened?*

The Major continues, holding the paper again. 'This says he entered the room of an elderly woman. Do you know anything about that?'

'Kevin wouldn't. It's a lie.'

His voice hardened. 'My staff don't lie, and I am sure the elderly woman isn't lying. We called the police and your friend disappeared. That's not the action of an innocent person, is it?' He sniffs as if something rotten has crawled up his nose. 'I'll not tolerate any behaviour that upsets our guests.'

'I wasn't here. I didn't do anything.'

Pinching his nose with forefinger and thumb, sighing, 'I know you weren't here, and that's the only reason I'm letting you stay. But, and I mean this young man, any trouble and I'll not hesitate to ask you to leave. Do you understand?' Relieved, you nod. 'Make sure you do. Good night.'

The Bun's eyes are scathing as you stand in front of her for a second time. 'Can I have a room now, please?'

She sneers. 'So, he's letting you stay. You should be out on the street.' Ignoring her comment. 'Four nights please?'

'That's one hundred and twenty-five dollars.'

Your mouth drops open. 'Uh, that's, that's more than last time.'

'Yes. Prices go up. Other people want these rooms.'

'Um. I can't.' Shaking your head. 'I haven't got that much.' Sniggering, 'Then go across the street. It's better suited to your type anyway. I'm busy.'

Your shoulders slump, beaten. 'Um, three nights then? Please?'

'What? Speak up.'

'Three nights.'

Glaring, her mouth open to say something, but thinking better of it, she snaps it shut. 'That's one hundred. You got that?'

Handing over the money, regretting giving away the five dollars. You reach to take the key from her fingers, she holds onto it, 'I'm watching you. Any problems, and you'll be out on your ear.'

The new room is identical to the previous one, faded linoleum, single door cupboard, and you bet the bed will creak, but this room also has a bedside table and clock radio. As you throw your bag across the room and watch it crash into the corner, you feel an overwhelming sense of despair, not helped when you empty your pockets onto the bed. *Two lousy tickets and a measly sixty cents, that's all I have.*

Could he have done what they said? There has to be an explanation. How will I find him now? You glare at the pitiful sum of money lying on the bed. *Maybe consider the stranger's idea?* Your gut says no. *I must find Kevin.* He mentioned something about a train. *But, where's the station?* The night drags on, and sleep is nowhere to be seen as you toss and turn, counting the minutes until morning.

≠

Wiping her hands down the front of her apron, face creasing into a smile, she doesn't appear to mind that you haven't bought anything. 'Which station, love? There's Town Hall, Wynyard and Central.'

Shrugging, not sure. You'd thought there was only one, and hoped Kevin would turn up and then everything would go back to the way it was before you left.

'Central's closest dear. Turn left out of the cafe and follow Pitt Street. You can't miss it.'

Your search for him begins in the snooker room, a single fluorescent tube flickers casting long shadows. Behind a counter a man who barely acknowledges your presence. Two other people are in the room. A boy engrossed in a game of snooker while a girl watches. His malicious smirk as he glances in your direction catches your attention—he fits the description of the Sharpies Kevin warned you about.

The girl leans over to whisper something to him, and peeks at you from below her black fringe. His reaction doesn't instil any confidence that they'll leave you alone—time to go. As you do, their laughter follows you down the stairs.

At Central Station, Kevin's absence worries you. *Will you see him again?* You push the thought aside and focus on the people getting off the arriving trains. There's a large number. *Bloody hell, why do they all get here at the same time?* Despite straining your eyes, you can't spot any sign of him or his distinctive red top hat among the crowd. Standing on a bench for a better view only attracts curious glances from passersby.

The station becomes quiet again as the minutes pass, with only tourists and railway workers milling about on the platforms. While waiting for the next train, you watch a flock of pigeons and their routine of circling the dome ceiling and then settling on the iron struts after each arrival and departure. *Dumb birds, they should be used to the noise by now. Maybe, like me, they have nowhere else to go?*

You shift uncomfortably on the wooden bench, knowing you can't leave yet. This is your last hope to find Kevin. The uncertainty, a weight in your stomach.

A woman heads in your direction, staggering from side to side, her eyes fixed on your bench. You hope she'll pass by, but instead sits, arranging a woollen coat over her knees. Tufts of grey poke from beneath a greasy Levi cap. Snuffling and coughing, taking a quick glance at you before she wipes her nose with the back of one hand, a toothless grin if it wasn't for the yellow solitary tooth. Mottled blue flesh shows through black stockings; a red sand shoe on one foot, white on the other. Pulling out a newspaper, she spreads it across the bench as if she's in a library. Looking away, you're only interested in the arrival of the next train, hoping the lady in the cafe is correct, that this is the best station.

A rattling sound signifies another train is arriving. *Will he be on this one?* The old lady sniffs and stands, putting on her coat, throwing a haughty look at you as she leaves. Watching her walk away, amused at the cap sitting at an angle on her head, giving her a youthful appearance. You sense she may have been a lady of means once, long ago. She leaves the newspaper behind. Your anticipation turns to a realisation that he's not going to magically appear. The disappointment grips you like a vice, squeezing the hope out of you. *How much longer can I bear this?* A gust of wind stirred by an arriving train flutters the old lady's discarded newspaper. You contemplate it for a moment, then, with a shrug, *why not?* You reach down and pick it up. *There could be something.*

Your hopes are dashed as you flick through page after page. There are jobs for bricklayers and factory workers in places you've never heard of. Your frustration builds, and you crumple the paper, ready to toss it away in disgust. But then, a headline catches your eye, and your heart skips a beat: "Dishwasher wanted for a leading city restaurant." *City restaurant.* The words ignite a spark of excitement.

Hastily, you smooth out the paper and read on—interviews at three pm on Tuesday at Albert's Restaurant,

Double Bay. Panic sets in as you realise that's today, and you don't have much time left to get there. The clock on the station wall already shows one. *Can I make it?*

Half an hour later, you find yourself increasingly desperate. *Where the fuck is Double Bay?* It's nowhere to be found on any of the train boards. *How the hell am I supposed to get there?* You look around frantically for help, finally spotting a ticket booth. Clutching your hands together, you hurry over, hoping the attendant can help you.

'Uh, can you tell me...?' your voice filled with anxiety.

Without looking up, the man in the booth snaps, 'Where to?'

'I want to go to Double Bay?'

He exhales, looking at you. 'Are you joking, son? Trains don't go to Double Bay.'

With a frustrated shake of your head, 'Oh. Uh, how can, how do I get there?'

'Catch a bus. You'll find 'em out front. Next.'

You remember seeing buses lined up at the entrance to the station. You hurry out, *I can't be late.* Ten minutes later there's still no sign of a bus that goes to Double Bay. Time is ticking. Watching a man dispensing tickets, you head over. 'A ticket to Double Bay, please?'

'No buses to Double Bay from here, son.'

Fuck. 'Where do I find one?'

He pauses, scanning your appearance. 'Double Bay's a bit posh. Have you got the right place?'

'I ... um, yes. I'm going for a job.'

'A job? Sure.' With a cold laugh, 'You have a job in Double Bay. Okay, I believe you. Thousands wouldn't. Go up Pitt Street.' Pointing back the way you'd come. 'To Park Street, near Hyde Park. Do you know where that is?' Nodding. Kevin and you had walked through Hyde Park on that first night. 'You'll find buses leaving for Double Bay from there.'

Thinking of the meagre sixty cents in your pocket, 'Uh, how much to get there?'

He taps his fingers on his chin and sighs. 'Not sure son, probably fifty cents.'

Nodding a thanks, relieved you have enough money, but now you've lost track of time. *I must get a hustle on.* You dash across Belmore Park, oblivious to a white sedan parked in the centre, its four occupants keenly observing you.

The bus winds along New South Head Road with picturesque views of high cliffs on one side and charming houses perched on the other. A Double Bay sign comes into view. You signal the bus to stop, grateful that you've arrived. But, panic sets in again when you get off and there are no shops in sight. *Did you get off too early?*

Heart racing, you start running, desperately hoping Double Bay isn't too far away, your chest tightens making breathing difficult.

With the clock ticking, exhausted, a Woolworths store appears around a bend. This must be it. Can't be far now. And then, with a sigh of relief you spot a sign pointing to Albert's Restaurant.

With sweat pouring down your face, you hesitate before entering. *Is it worth going in the way I look?*

The idea of Kevin returning feels like an elusive dream, but one you can't let go of. Right now, you need a job. Pushing through the door, reveals a polished timber floor that shines deep black, complimenting an oak bar adorned with brass railings, a man standing behind it, polishing glasses. Beyond, an archway, tables draped in pristine white cloth and surrounded by plush red velvet chairs.

Feeling that you stand out like a sore thumb in this place, you turn to leave, the man stops polishing. 'Can I help you?'

His question hangs in the air.

Throat dry, you turn back and face him. 'Uh, I came about, about the job.'

'What?'

'The dishwashing job.'

'Oh. That. I'm afraid I've already offered it to someone.'

'Oh.'

'You ok? Do you need to sit down? You look like you might collapse.'

'No. I'm ... I'm fine.' Hiding your disappointment, you reach for the door handle.

The man puts the glass down. 'Hang on. Wait, wait a minute. Do you need the job that badly?'

'Umm, I need a job. That's all.' Tears prick at the corners of your eyes. You must get away.

'How long have you been looking?' Wanting to run out of the door, instead you mutter, 'I've just started.'

'You sure you're alright?'

'Yes. I'm fine.'

'When was your last meal? I mean a decent one.'

'Uh ...' The memory of Gordon's curry floods your taste buds, and you're barely able to refrain from licking your lips. 'I'm okay, really.'

His eyes soften. 'Look, I can't do anything about the job. But I can offer you a meal. So come and sit down. It's on me.'

'Are you sure?'

He throws the cloth on the bar, glances in the mirror and straightens his bow tie. 'Have a seat. I'm Richard, the manager. We're closed, but the chef's still here. I'll get him to cook you a steak. How's that?'

≠

Sitting in a velvet chair, running your hands over the crisp white tablecloth. *What would his customers say if they saw me here?*

Richard returns. 'It won't be long. Let me make you one of my favourite drinks. That'll cheer you up.' He reappears, holding a glass filled with a crystal-clear liquid, a slice of lemon gently floating on its surface. With a warm smile, he places the drink on the table, announcing, 'It's a gin and tonic. I'll be in the bar if you need anything.' As he turns to leave, he pauses, meticulously inspecting the back of a nearby chair, before casually flicking a piece of fluff away and sniffing.

You can't help but notice the faint bitterness of the drink as you peer over the rim of the glass at a woman approaching, gliding across the carpeted floor. Steam rises from a plate she carries. 'Hello. I see you have Richard's favourite drink. He does love his gin and tonics.'

Feeling embarrassed, you shyly reply, 'I don't think I do.'

Her laughter is sweet as she reassures you, 'It's an acquired taste, much like Richard. So, what's your story?'

Her manner is comforting and perhaps due to the gin and tonic you open up about the trip, and Danny leaving. You omit the part about Kevin. 'I came here for the dishwasher job, but it's gone. He offered me a meal. It's kind of him.'

She winks, 'It certainly is. Enjoy.'

The plate contains a mouthwatering steak covered in a rich, dark sauce and a generous portion of carrots and potatoes. You remember Kevin's words about not knowing when your next meal will be. Wise words, as you enjoy every bite. As you finish the last sip of your gin and tonic, you lean back with a contented smile appreciating the comfort of a full stomach.

The lady returns. 'I take it you enjoyed that?' she says, picking up the empty plate. Before you can reply, she replaces it with a folded twenty-dollar note. 'This is for you,' she insists warmly, 'Take care.'

'Uh, oh, I don't know if I can pay you back.'

'No need. I know what it's like to be broke.'

Richard holds onto your hand as he says goodbye, but he does offer you some hope, with a dry smile, he says, 'Come back if you need help and I'll see what I can do.'

Settling into your seat on the bus, smiling to yourself. You won't need Richard. *Everything's going to be alright.*

≠

You don't want to leave, but you have no choice? The hours of waiting have brought nothing but a cold bum and a stiff back. A voice inside insists that he's not coming back, ever. Once again, you consider the offer from the strange man that smelt of rotting vegetables. The idea of just talking to him scared the shit out of you, let alone doing what he suggested. *But, if it's the only way ...* Shuddering, you head back to the Palace.

Shading your eyes, darting across the street, dodging cars, annoyed drivers blasting their horns. Pausing at the edge of the park, you notice the stationary white car, something niggles in the back of your mind, dismissing it, head down, you plod across the park—you've decided to see if the old man turns up again. A feeling suggests he might.

A chill creeps through your body as the sun goes behind a veil of clouds and you regret not wearing your vest to shield from the cold. Deep in thought, you suddenly stop. Your heart skips a beat. The white car is obstructing your path. *What's it doing here?*

Four burly men emerge. Their sheer size and intense stares send a shiver down your spine. They move as one towards you, eight hard, unblinking eyes. A finger, fat like a pork sausage points. 'Your name Robinson?'

In sheer terror, you feel the urgent need to relieve yourself. As one approaches, brandishing a badge—shouting, 'We're police officers.' Their stony expressions leave you shaken, and thoughts of speaking with the old man or searching for Kevin shatter. *How does he know my name?* Nodding, straining to stop from wetting yourself.

Another one steps closer, as you back away. 'We want to talk to you. You're staying at the People's Palace, is that correct?' You nod, unsure if you can form words, your mouth dry, throat slammed shut. 'We're looking for a boy called Kevin. He's a friend of yours, isn't he?'

'I ... he ...'

Interrupting, one points back towards the railway station. 'What were you doing in there? Waiting for a train?' He laughs, the sound is cold comfort.

Shoving your hands into your pockets so they don't see them shake, 'I. Oh, I. I was ... waiting for ...' Words fail. *What else can I say?*

'Waiting? Waiting for fuckin' what?'

'Umm.'

'Is umm all you have to say? You a fuckin' idiot?'

Another sneers. 'We asked what the fuck you were doing in there. This Kevin, he assaulted an old woman. Did you enjoy watching?'

One of them near the rear door, bigger than the others, his belly hiding the belt around his pants, shouts, 'Say something you little shit.'

'He, he wouldn't.'

'He wouldn't, huh? Did you meet Kevin in there?' Nodding towards the station, 'Maybe gloat over what the two of you did?' His hand smacks down on the car, startling you, 'Speak up.' Unable to meet his gaze, you stare at the ground. 'Did you? Or are you planning something else?'

Could they know about the other man? Voice shaking, 'No. I. He. I didn't.'

The man closest to you seizes your arm. 'You're coming with us.'

You resist, trying to break free. 'Why? Where are you taking me? Your heart pounds.

His grip intensifies, sneering, 'Because we damn well say so.' Beads of sweat glisten on his unshaven cheeks.

You struggle to escape, tears welling up. Frightened, you shout, 'I haven't done anything. I don't know where Kevin is.'

'Enough. Get in the car. We want to look at your room,' he retorts, holding the door open. Passersby avoid eye contact, unwilling to get involved. Some shake their heads in disgust.

The officer with the big belly sits on your left, and another on your right. The vehicle smells of stale hamburgers and cigarette smoke mixed with sweat. Sandwiched in the seat, you close your eyes in silent prayer. The police radio crackles, and the officer behind the wheel grumbles as he leans across and turns it off. Your bladder, let's go.

'How long have you known this, Kevin?' the large man asks, his stomach wobbling each time the car hits a bump.

'I ... um, a few days.'

'You meet him at the People's Palace?' You nod. 'Were you with him when he assaulted the old woman?'

'No. He wouldn't hurt anyone. He's not like that.'

'Is that right? You know that after a few days, do you?' A ghoulish imitation of a grin on his face. 'I bet you both enjoyed it.'

The car comes to a halt in the middle of Pitt Street, opposite the Palace. They get out, one leans back into the car, his face inches from yours, 'Get the fuck out. I want to see your room. Now!'

You whine, 'I haven't done anything.'

With a firm grip on your shirt collar, he pulls you out of the car. His face twists in disgust at the sharp smell of urine. He raises his hand to strike you but refrains, noticing the curious glances from people on the street. Instead, clasping the back of your neck, he steers you across the road and up the steps of the Palace.

Inside, the Bun smirks as she watches you being marched through the foyer, her grin widening with each step. A knowing nod between her and one of them confirms your suspicions. The anger towards her intensifies. *It's her fault. The bitch.*

'Take us to your room,' the man with his hand around your neck demands, and your heart races, scared of what might happen when you reach the room. He tightens his grip momentarily before releasing you as you fumble to find the key. 'Give it here.' A nearby guest in a bathrobe, wet hair dripping, hurries past, looking the other way. They shove you inside.

'How long have you been here?'

'A few nights. I'm moving out as soon as I find a job.'

'No job?' Your heart stops. *Shit, keep your fuckin mouth shut.*

Picking your bag up, tipping the contents onto the bed, they paw through it. The cowboy vest hangs over the end of the bed and one picks it up, examining it. 'Did you steal this?' The tickets fall out and flutter to the floor. 'What are these?' He picks them up, swiping you across the face. 'Where did you get them?'

Holding your cheek, sullen, you mumble. 'I, uh, someone gave them to me.'

'Who'd give you these? I bet a bob to nothing that you stole them.' He tucks them away. 'I'll keep them,' patting his pocket.

The large one lets out a long slow whistle. 'Well, well, well. What do we have here?' He's holding your Bowie knife. Your stomach drops to your toes. *Shit. Shit.* You'd forgotten all about it. 'Is this yours?' Gulping, you nod. 'Why do you have a knife?'

'To ... to protect me.'

He lets out a snort. 'From what, old women?' Sliding it out of its sheaf, it catches the light, shining wickedly in his hand. 'Have you used it?' Your legs wobble a shake of your head. *Will they put me in jail?*

The large one growls, 'You're lucky kid. The manager confirmed you weren't here. But take this as a warning. Stay out of trouble and away from this Kevin character ... or else.' One tucks the cowboy vest under his arm. 'I'll keep this.'

'And this,' says the beer belly, putting the knife under his jacket. 'Can't have you wandering around our fair city with it.'

Stopping at the door, he turns around. 'It would be best if you crawled back under the rock you came from. If we see you again ...' The threat hangs in the air as the door closes with a thud.

Curled-up on your bed, you let out an uncontrollable scream.

Her footsteps echo across the lobby as she pounds towards you, arms swinging. Her blue dress billows like a tent in a wind tunnel. *If I can make it to the stairs, I'll be okay.* But she blocks the way, legs planted, chest heaving, and gasps. 'The Major ...' A wheeze. 'Wants ...' Another gasp. You are hoping she collapses to the floor, pitying the floor. 'Wants to see you.' Florid cheeks puff as she exhales.

'Can I see him tomorrow?'

Regaining her breath, she pulls herself up to her full height, four feet at least in your estimation. 'No. He said when you came back.' You look towards the office door, then at the stairs. She's won.

'You wanted to see me?'

The Major looks up from his newspaper, then places it down on the desk. Thin fingers cup his chin as his watery eyes roam up and down your face. The hair on the back of your neck stands on end. His voice, barely a whisper carries across the room. 'The police. What did they want?'

Fuck, she must've told him. 'Umm, nothing. Wanted to see my room, that's all.'

'Why?'

A shrug. 'I don't know.'

'Police don't inspect a person's room for no reason.'

'They asked about Kevin.'

'Do you remember what I said last time?' He didn't wait for a reply. 'I told you I didn't want any trouble. Police dragging a resident through our lobby is the sort of thing I was talking about.'

'They didn't ...'

Interrupting, 'This Kevin.' He spat the name out as if there was a nasty taste in his mouth. 'He's caused enough trouble already. I don't want anymore. I want you to leave in the morning.'

'I didn't do anything.' The whine in your voice pisses you off. 'I've got two nights left. I'll go after that. Please. I've got nowhere to go.'

His lips press together. 'Beth will refund one night. Consider yourself lucky. She recommended we put you out tonight.'

Sniffing, you mutter, 'I bet. This isn't fair.'

Picking up his paper, flicking it open, dismissing you.

The Bun's grin lingers on her face as you hurry past, racing up the stairs to your room. Collapsing onto the bed, a flood of memories rush in—the Vic hotel, a Valiant speeding down East Point Road, the coconut tree, the tense hours in the emergency room. A shiver seizes you. *Why's everything so fuckin' hard?*

Distressed, you wake clutching the pillow. Your legs hang over the edge of the bed, the soles of your feet are blackened and caked with dirt. One big toe throbs. A faint memory lingers—a blurry image of stumbling down a hallway, accidentally kicking an empty bucket sending it rattling across the floor followed by a squeaking of bed springs and a grumbling female voice.

Then, a rooftop swims into view, a howling wind, your flannelette shirt, tight around your shoulders no match for the gale. You regret not having your buckskin vest.

A metal door bangs closed. Glancing around, no one else nearby. It won't matter soon, anyway. Below, the city lights twinkle like Christmas decorations. The stench of garbage and car fumes drifts up from the street—your nose wrinkles. Hand shaking you take the slip of paper from your pocket, knowing nobody would care even if they got to read it. In frustration, you tear the paper into strips and release them into the air, they're carried away by the wind across the city skyline. The door bangs again, but you pay it no attention, something else is on your mind.

Your cheeks are damp despite the rain having stopped. With a sigh, you move toward the rooftop's edge, your body heavy with a sense of despair. A sudden trembling takes over, and you collapse to the ground in overwhelming fear.

What happened? Shaking your head, the images fade. You're unsure of what you've seen. A scrap of paper stuck to your jeans is the only reminder. Sniffling, you know you have to leave. *Where will I go?*

Richard's words, *come back if you need help and I'll see what I can do.* You know he'll help, but ... You felt the tension in him, like a coiled spring. *Tension is wrong. Secrets, that's it, his secrets.* The lady said he was an acquired taste. *What the fuck does that mean?*

An initial sense of relief brings a smile as you discover that the Bun isn't occupying the booth. However, it's short-lived as a much larger woman is in the booth. Her expression stern as she surveys the lobby as if the entire area is exclusively hers.

Her canary-yellow dress struggles to contain her ample breasts, which quiver with every movement. With a shake of the head, breasts jiggling. 'We don't give refunds.'

'But the Major said I'd get one night back.'

Stay here,' she replied. With a bounce in her step, she crosses the floor to the office, knocks on the door and enters without waiting for an invitation.

After a wait of five minutes, she returns, clearly flustered. 'Well,' she huffs, squeezing herself back into the booth, 'The Major says to provide a refund for one night. Consider yourself fortunate.' With a dismissive sniff, she thrusts ten dollars in your direction. 'Take this, and don't return. Your kind is not welcome here.'

You contemplate arguing for the full refund, but glancing at her expression makes you reconsider. Leaving without looking back, you know you can't have anything to do with the man or the place across the street. It has to be Richard.

≠

Your shirt sticks to your back, water drips from your chin as you wait to cross George Street. You look longingly at the brightly lit shops. *Could I hang out there until I go see Richard?* A soft voice interrupts.

'Hello.' The owner has a set of perfectly straight teeth and blonde hair. A clipboard in one hand; the other playing with a strand of her golden locks.

'Uh, um, hi.'

'You going somewhere?' Her head inclines towards the bag slung over your shoulder.

'Yeah, I'm meeting friends.'

'Where do they live?'

'Who?'

'Your friends, silly.'

'Oh them. You know ... around.'

'I'm with a group that helps people who are lost. Are you lost?'

'Am I what?'

'Lost.'

Confused, shaking your head, 'No, I haven't been in Sydney long, that's all.'

She grins, her eyes dancing in delight. Her fingers continue to twirl a strand of her blonde hair. With a frown. 'I don't mean lost in Sydney. Can I ask you some questions? We can go over there, out of the rain.' Walking ahead, she stands under an awning, waiting, pencil in her hand. The mannequins unmoved by her beauty, watch unblinking. The pencil taps on the clipboard, a sign to you that she's serious. 'What's your name?'

'It's umm, Graham.'

'How old are you?'

'Fourteen.'

'What are you doing here?'

What can I say that won't sound odd after all that's happened? You tell her as much as you dare, deciding not to talk about Kevin or the incident.

'You're having quite an adventure, aren't you? Would you like to meet my friends?'

'Your friends?' You look around, expecting them to suddenly appear.

There's a sweet tinkling sound from her mouth and you shiver. 'Not here. At our church. It's not far.' She smiles, glancing at your soaked clothes. 'It's warm and dry. And there's hot food. You'll like it, I promise.'

You nod in agreement, following as she heads back towards Pitt Street keeping a watchful eye out for white cars. She leads the way along Hunter, then turns into Castlereagh Street, you pick up your pace so you can keep up with her. Eventually, she stops in front of two imposing timber doors and without hesitation, pulls one open and enters. Pausing, you are able to make out the letters *SC* and *Y* above the doors.

To your surprise, you find no signs of a traditional church inside. A large trestle table holds stainless steel containers emitting steam from their lids. Another table has stacks of small red-bound books, but they don't interest you.

An eerie glow from a blue and green stained-glass window at the back of the hall illuminates the room. A group of people are seated at a small table, and you hear clapping coming from behind a door. The blonde girl points towards a timber rack. 'Put your bag down and get food. Then I'll introduce you to the Supervisor.'

Before you can ask what she means, the girl disappears.

Glancing at the wall clock, worried. It's already past twelve. But the aromas in the room make your mouth water, hurrying over to the steaming containers, lifting the lids your stomach somersaults with delight as you fill your plate with stew and potatoes, ignoring the carrots. *Ugh*. With a plate in hand, you join the others at the table. As you settle down to eat, the blonde girl returns.

'Come and meet the Supervisor.'

You look up at her. 'What's your name?'

'We don't use names here. We're all brother and sister.' With a flick of her hair, she indicates for you to accompany her. At the end of the hall, you enter a room that's longer than it is wide, reminding you of a food pantry. The sparse room contains a grey metal desk and a picture on the wall of a figure on a white cloud, that's all, except for the man with his back to the door. He turns around and smiles.

'Hello sister. Who's this then?'

'Supervisor, he's a fellow traveller. I wanted you to meet him.'

'Of course.' His voice is soft. Eyes sunk into a skull that is topped by bushy eyebrows and a ridged forehead. 'And what brings you to our modest group?' He sighs as he asks, as if needing to pose the question but not caring for the answer.

'She did.' You nod towards the girl, who's standing at attention, hands clasped in front of her chest.

'I mean would you say you're lost?'

A prickle on the back of your neck. *Lost. She said that too.* A voice inside you shouts, *Get out of here!* 'No. No, I'm not lost. It's my first time here.'

A laugh erupts, but it's dry, without humour. His head moves from side to side, then forward, like a bobble-head toy.

'I don't mean here in the city. In your heart, your soul. Are you aware of our church?'

You try to be polite. 'I ... umm ...'

He continues as if you're not in the room, a rapturous look on his face: 'We help souls find the Supreme Being.'

'The what?' The words come out harsher than you intended.

Tutting, he clasps his hands behind his back, as if he's about to give a sermon, chest pushed forward, head lifted, with a distant look in his eyes. 'Many are disbelievers. Here we seek one's true spiritual nature.'

'I'm meeting my friends.'

He nods. 'Sister, let's show this traveller our friendship.'

She smiles and opens the door. The meeting with the Supervisor is over. As you leave the room, she whispers, 'The Supervisor likes you. It's unusual to be invited in straight away.'

You give her a thin smile. *He's creepy, and I don't want an invitation.* Memories of your mother's fascination with church surface.

≠

Every Sunday, your mother, wearing a black dress and pearl necklace, heads to Sunday service. After church, she was careful not to crease the dress, hanging it up and storing away the pearls. Then she reverted back to her usual self.

A mother who, for all her torment, tried to keep you out of harm's way, although when exasperated she would utter the words you dreaded, 'Wait until your father gets home.'

The day that is clear in your mind is the one with the brussel sprouts. She was in a foul mood that day. Not only do you not like brussel sprouts but, compounding your dislike, one had the cheek to roll off your plate and land on the floor with a plop during Sunday lunch. Your mother, eyes glittering, yells, 'Don't play with your food.'

You smirk, forgetting that it is absolutely the wrong thing to do once her Irish temper is up. 'Stop it.' Her hand draws back, and she hurls the knife she's holding. It slices across the top of your head. Blood spurts out, red rivulets run down the side of your face. She wails, although it is you that is hurt, her face ashen and wraps a towel around your head, bundling you into your sister's baby carriage. Its enormous wheel's bounce wildly as she rushes you along Shenley Street to the hospital.

No, religion is not something you care for.

≠

The girl is still talking. 'Once you prove yourself and are a loyal follower, we'll have more time together.'

She smiles, and it melts your heart, but the words worry you. *Prove yourself?* She heads towards a room with singing coming from it. You stay where you are. 'I'll come back. After I meet my friends.'

Halting, turning around, hands on hips, barking, 'You must join now. It'll help you find your way.'

'I'll come back soon, promise. But I must go.'

'If you're a follower, you'll stay and get to know me.'

Heart beating faster, you beg, 'Please.' She throws you a condescending stare and stamps off. It reminds you of another blonde haired girl.

Your nerves tingle with anticipation as car after car pulls up, dropping off children who run up the steps and into the picture theatre, laughing and yelling. You're eagerly awaiting her arrival, hoping she won't leave you standing here much longer. You blame Scott, as you didn't believe him when he said Shelley liked you.

She's the prettiest girl in school, with soulful eyes and untamed, wild blonde hair that swirls around her head. One afternoon after school, she'd approached you and asked if you wanted to go to the Saturday matinee with her. Nervously, you stammer out a yes. She giggles, squeezing your hand before rejoining her friends, who were curious about the boy she'd been talking to.

Now, you wonder where she is.

'Hello,' a familiar voice interrupts your thoughts. You whirl around to find Shelley standing there. Her lips curved into a coy smile. 'Did you think I wasn't coming?'

Your face flushes with embarrassment, trying to cover it up. 'No, I... never doubted you'd come,' you manage to say, your heart thuds loud enough for her to hear.

She laughs, a light, airy sound that makes your heart flutter. Then, without warning, she kisses you on the lips, the taste of raspberry lingers as the movie begins.

Climb Every Mountain echoed through the theatre as the movie came to a close. Shelley gets up and hurries towards the exit. You try to keep up, but the crowded aisles hinder your progress. Once outside, you see her talking to another boy, and your heart sinks as you watch her kiss him. Despair wells up, and you can't help but call out her name. The boy turns around–it's Scott.

Snatching your bag, you rush outside onto Castlereagh Street. It's time to go see Richard, and find out if he meant what he said. Unsure what it'll mean for you.

Part Three: Desire

E verything appears unchanged. *What did I expect?* Only two days have passed since you stood in this very spot. Richard, is in the same place, polishing glasses. He pauses, sets the glass on the bar, and scrutinises you. 'Well, look what the cat has dragged in.' Tossing a cloth your way. 'Here. Dry yourself off. So, what brings you back to my humble establishment?'

Teeth chattering, water pooling at your feet spreading across the polished timber floor, 'I ...' Stopping, as a girl bounces into the room, coming to a halt as she glances at Richard and then at you. 'Everything okay Richard?'

'Yep. This is a friend of mine.' He flicks his wrist at her in a dismissive manner. Sniffing, the girl leaves, slamming the door behind her. 'Sorry about that. You were saying?'

'Uh, you said you might help me. If I ...' Lowering your eyes, unable to meet his gaze. *This is stupid.* 'I understand if you can't. I'll go.'

'Wait. What's happened?'

'I need ...' Looking at the water surrounding your feet. 'I've got nowhere else to go.'

You glance up to see how your statement has been received. His eyes have a faraway look, as if he's considering something. *I shouldn't have come. He won't help.* 'My mum,' he says, pausing, 'God rest her soul.

Always said you should keep your word. I can put you up for a few nights.'

'Thank you. It's only until I find, I mean, meet my friend.'

'Alright. Let me finish here. Then we'll go.' Turning away, he picks up another glass, vigorously wiping it while humming. After a thorough inspection, he approves and places it on a shelf. As you watch, uncertain what to do next, you wonder if he's forgotten about you. There are the velvet-covered chairs to sit on, but that doesn't seem right in your wet clothes, so you stay where you are while he fusses with the glasses. Then, wiping the bar down with a grand sweeping gesture, he steps back to admire his work. Finally, he says, 'Okay, let's get out of here. The car's out back. Go through the kitchen.'

You hesitate, glancing towards the restaurant. 'It's okay. Everyone's gone.' He walks over and puts an arm around your shoulders, when you stiffen, he withdraws it, casting a cautious glance at you from the corner of his eye.

'Go through there,' pointing to the kitchen door. 'I'll put on the alarm.'

You push open a steel door and step into a walled courtyard. The stench of rotting food is overwhelming. *What a waste.* Richard, close behind, takes hold of your arm. 'C'mon. It's this way.' He guides you across the courtyard to a blue car, the interior refreshing after the rotting vegetables. 'It's only the cat and me at home,' he says, pulling into the street. 'Hope you'll feel comfortable.'

Once again you concentrate on the streets; you'll need to find your way back to Central. *I can't give up on Kevin. Not yet.*

Richard, in a high falsetto, announces, 'Here we are.' Surprised, you glance across at him, wondering once more if you're doing the right thing.

He gracefully bows as he opens the front door. 'Welcome to my abode.' You try to figure out what he means, and smile. A cat dashes down the hallway, its claws tapping on the wooden floor before gracefully stopping by his side. Gently you run your hand along its back, it purrs contentedly. Richard chuckles with delight. 'She's taken a liking to you.' The cat leaps onto a hall table, basking in the afternoon sunlight, a gleam in its eyes brings back a haunting memory.

≠

It happened during your family's stay on a farm owned by Boer friends of your father's. One evening, their twin boys, Matties and Janco, invite you and your brother to join them on a hunt.

'We're gonna get these fuckin' hares that eat all the maize,' Janco says, smirking. 'Ag man, wear strong takkies.'

Janco is big for a sixteen-year-old. His nugget-shaped head rests like a boulder on top of his broad shoulders. He boasts of his prowess on the rugby field, bragging he's the first junior invited to play in the men's team.

We pile into a battered Ford pick-up equipped with a spotlight that Matties switches on. 'This is how we find those bastards.' Janco, carrying his beloved .303 Mauser, places it on the rack inside the rear window, grinning at your reaction. 'In case we see other fukkers or more kudu,' he says, getting behind the wheel.

The mention of kudu brings back when you saw that gun in action. Shortly after arriving, the families were enjoying a picnic in a dry riverbed. Fresh watermelon spread out on the hood of the Ford when a majestic kudu bull emerged from the bushes, its impressive spiral horns shining as black as night in the sunlight. Janco retrieved the Mauser from the rack, sweeping the discarded watermelon peels away with one hand, he rests his elbows on the hood and takes aim. The rifle cracked, but the kudu remained still. You felt relief, thinking he'd missed the shot. However, moments later, blood gushes from the kudu's nostrils, its front legs buckle as it collapses to the ground.

Janco and Matties, cheering excitedly, rush toward the dying animal with knives drawn. Matties, hands deep in the kudu's belly, declaring, 'This is dinner.' Shocked by the violence, you stare at the kudu's lifeless eyes, its long eyelashes fluttering in the light wind, no longer a magnificent animal, now reduced to mere slabs of meat, as the sand in the riverbed turns pink.

≠

The Ford lurches over dried wheel ruts, you and your brother in the rear tray are thrown from side to side like old wheat-chaff bags. The spotlight searches the bush for hares. Laughing, Matties yells, 'Man, I love this. When the light hits these fukkers they freeze. Stupid bastards. Then we go stomp on 'em.' His eyes shine with excitement. Looking across at your brother, the question in your eyes. *What does he mean, stomp on them?*

Matties whoops: the light has captured two hares in its beam and they're frozen to the spot, their sides quivering. As the Ford skids to a stop, Janco jumps out and races forward, kicking and stomping on the hares in a mad frenzy. Blood and fur flies, the hares squeal. Janco makes his way back to the Ford and hurls the carcasses at your feet. 'We give 'em to the blacks,' he cries.

It's not long before Matties shouts again, the sound you're dreading. 'This one's for you rooineks,' he screams above the wind.

Legs trembling, heart racing, you and your brother cautiously descend from the truck's rear, aware that

Matties is observing your every step. In the distance, a hare is entangled in the sharp thorns of an acacia tree, desperately attempting to break free. Its eyes gleam as you approach, its movements more frantic, driving itself deeper into the thorny trap. You share a nervous glance with your brother—his face mirrors your fear.

When you look back at Matties, illuminated by the spotlight, his eyes are fixed on you. With a deep breath, you turn your attention back to the trapped hare, understanding what needs to be done.

≠

'Let me show you the bedroom.' Taking your elbow, Richard leads you down a hallway with black and white photos of men in various stages of undress on the wall. A chilling shiver of fear courses through your stomach like frozen ice. 'Here's your boudoir.' More words you don't understand, but no smile, your chest is clamped tight. 'I hope you find it comfortable.' Flinging the door open to a room not much bigger than the one at the Palace. There are timber bunk beds against the wall but nothing else, not even a rug on the floor. 'Take the top or bottom bunk.' He winks. 'I prefer the bottom.'

Missing the innuendo, 'The bottom's fine.'

His eyes linger on your face, and then, with a wave, 'Put your things down and I'll start dinner. Quick and easy tonight, like me.' Laughing as he goes to leave, then stopping, 'Take a shower. You could do with one.'

Peeling off your clothes, tired to the bone, you drop them on the bathroom floor, making a muddy pile on the pristine white tiles. *I'll pick them up after the shower.* You've noticed Richard's fastidious ways and don't want to upset him. The hot water soaks into your pores, washing the cold away, but not the dread. You can't stop thinking about whether you're doing the right thing. *What choice do I have?* Stepping out of the shower, eyes full of lather, groping for the towel, sure that you placed it within easy reach. As you wipe the soap away, you see Richard standing in the doorway, the towel in his hand. A cold spasm slithers down your back. 'Uh, can I have the towel please?'

'I see your clothes are on the floor. There's a basket.' He nudges the wet clothes with his foot, still holding onto the towel.

'Can I ...?' He throws it towards you, turns and leaves without another word. Wrapping it around your waist, you fight back tears. *What have I done?* You hear banging in the kitchen, then he shouts, 'Dinner's nearly ready. How about some help?' Pulling on a dry T-shirt and a pair of shorts, you reluctantly go into the kitchen.

Richard is all smiles, handing you knives and forks, his fingers brushing against yours. 'Hurry up, we don't want dinner going cold, do we dear boy.' He relaxes during dinner, talking about himself, the restaurant, and life in Sydney. He mentions Oxford Street. 'Do you know where that is?' Shaking your head, you have no idea. He pauses, takes a deep breath and eyes you for a moment, coming to a decision, he mumbles, 'You understand that I like men, don't you?' You eye your plate. 'Is that a problem?' You shake your head; eyes fixed on the plate. Richard continued, 'Tell me about you? How did you end up in my restaurant?'

Relieved that he's changed the subject, you break into a lengthy explanation of the trip and meeting Kevin. But, avoid any mention of the police or that he has disappeared.

'Won't someone miss you?'

'I doubt it. No-one cares.'

'I'm sure that's not true. You can stay here for a few nights, so make yourself at home until you sort something out.' He stands and walks around the table his index finger trails across the surface. Stopping behind you and picking up your plate, his hot breath against your cheek.

Edging away, you blurt out, 'Let me do the dishes. I can do that.'

Richard titters. 'That's right. You're a dishwasher.'

Debating whether you can slink off to bed after you finish the washing up, deciding you can't, you join him in the lounge room. *After all, he is helping me.* He's on the lounge, the cat on his lap. 'Sorry about earlier. I find it stressful having a young man under my roof.' Fanning himself with his hand, 'I'd rather have him under me.' He giggles and pushes the cat off, sliding across the yellow lounge towards you.

Your throat closes; it's hard to breathe. *No, not again.* You stutter, 'Should, should I ... I go?'

Shaking his head, 'No. I like the company.' His leg presses against yours. 'I get lonely.' The pressure increases.

Moving away, you mumble, 'I can't. Sorry, I ...'

'Very well. Time for bed. There's a front-door key on the table.'

Climbing into bed, you're glad he left you alone. The queasiness in your stomach eases. *Maybe this will work out. But I can't, couldn't ...* Sighing. *I've gotta find Kevin.*

The door slowly opens, and a faint light seeps into your room from the hallway. Standing in the doorway is Richard, his body tense, resembling a tightly wound violin string, there's a sense of anticipation surrounding him. His erection is obvious. 'I like you,' he whispers, 'And I think you owe me something, for helping you out.'

'I, I never ...' A lump in your throat.

'What if I suck you off?'

Gritting your teeth. 'No. I ... I can't.'

His shoulders slump. He stares at you for a minute as if deciding what to do next, then turns on his heel. 'I'm away this weekend. Stay until then,' he says, as he leaves.

You want to explain, to tell him what happened. The door closes with a bang.

≠

Trusting a stranger was a desperate move driven by having no money and nowhere to sleep—the need to survive, making you agree to anything to have a roof over your head.

Staying in Sydney comes with a growing risk. Returning to Darwin wasn't an option. A strange feeling washes over you as you look back—a sense of being protected, though you can't explain how. During those moments, the consequences of your actions were the furthest from your mind. You defied the odds, surviving situations where the odds were against you.

Yet, there was one incident in Cape Town when you were seven, where luck nearly ran out for you.

A group of kids gathered outside a cinema after a Saturday morning matinee. A boy had been hit by a car while dashing into the road. Concerned onlookers gathered around, trying to help.

During the commotion, a man beside you suggested fetching a blanket from his flat to assist the boy. Asking you to accompany him. Without thinking you agree. When you arrive at the flat, there's another man in the bedroom, smoothing the bed sheets with one hand while the other is behind his back. The room is ripe, with a sour vinegar smell.

Escape seems unlikely as the man who brought you stands in the doorway.

The conversation turns to African witch doctors and the idea of *pointing the bone.* Your curiosity prompts questions that you shouldn't have asked. Then, with a shake of his head, the other man sent an unspoken signal. The man who brought you took you by the wrist and led you to the front door, the blanket nowhere in sight. A chilling reminder of how quickly a child can disappear, even within a crowd of people.

≠

A flash of red catches your attention—*or did it?* You've held onto hope for so long that doubt now assails you. *Was it Kevin or my imagination?* Shaking off uncertainty, you hastily leave the station, finding yourself on Elizabeth Street, trying to catch your breath. *Was it him?*

With disappointment, you lower your head, realising that you allowed yourself to believe your problems, for a fleeting moment, may be over and you'd be free from

Richard. Though you can't quite fathom how Kevin might help, you believe he will.

As you prepare to head back to the station, you collide with an older man who shoots you a disapproving look. Apologising under your breath, you cast a final glance along Elizabeth Street, then, something strikes the back of your head, and a familiar voice rings out. 'Where the fuck have you been?'

Turning around, mouth open, screaming, 'Kevin.' You wrap your arms around him in a bear hug.

'Easy, you'll crush me.'

Embarrassed, you step back, studying him at arm's length. His blonde hair is in a familiar tangle, his top hat in his left hand. 'I didn't think I'd ever see you again.' The weight of a mountain lifts from your shoulders.

'I would've come sooner but ...' A rueful smile crosses his face. 'I couldn't go near the Palace.'

'What the fuck happened with you? The bastards kicked me out.'

Kevin, ashen faced, 'What? Why?'

'They reckon I had something to do with it. The police grabbed me and looked at my room.' A pained expression crosses your face remembering them marching you across the foyer. 'They warned me to stay away from you. Then the prick in charge said I gotta go. Geez, I'm glad you're back.'

Shaking his head, 'I'm sorry. I went into the wrong room. This old bird began screaming at the top of her lungs ...' He paused. 'I pissed myself and ran. I went back after the hag in the booth left and got my stuff.' He glanced around and leant closer. 'I've got good news.'

'What? What news?'

'I'm staying in a boarding house, and there's a bed for you if you want it.'

You grab him and shake his arm. 'What? How? Tell me?'

People begin to stare. He put a finger to his lips. 'Shhh. Come over here.' The two of you huddle in a corner, whispering like conspirators.

'So where is this place? How can I live there?'

'Jesus. Stop shaking my fuckin' arm and I'll tell you.'

Sheepishly, you let go. 'Well?'

He grins. 'It's a boarding house for boys, boys like us, with nowhere else to live. It's in Lakemba. I told the lady who runs it about you and she said there's a bed if you want it. It's thirty-five a week.'

His words tumble out too fast to follow, until he mentions the money, then your shoulders sag. 'I ain't got that.'

'Can you get it?'

The old man's proposal flickers in the back of your mind. 'Who's gonna give me money?' Then you recall Reg's parting words. *Did he mean it?* Smiling, you look at Kevin. 'I might be able to get it.'

'You're not thinking about that old prick from the Palace, are you?'

'Fuck off, I'm not stupid.'

'Yes, you are. What then?'

'We met this bloke on the way to Sydney. His name's Reg. He said I should go see him if I needed anything. He works at … umm, shit.' Burying your head in your hands, *Fuck, where was it?* 'I can't remember.'

'Did he tell you a street, or anything about it, where he lived or worked?'

'Yes, where he worked. Said he had his dream job making beer, and I'd find him at a pub nearby, bell something.'

Kevin looked thoughtful. 'A brewery?'

'Maybe. I think so.'

'I've heard of Resch's brewery, in Redfern. Can't be that many pubs near it. Let's go see Betty. Don't tell her you ain't got the money. Tell her you're getting it from a friend.' Your heart swells as you look at Kevin, confident that everything will work out.

≠

As the train rattles along the tracks, the scenery transforms the further you get from the city. Dilapidated houses with windows and walls covered in soot and grime start to dominate the landscape.

You wonder if you'll get the money. *Will Reg help?* Asking Richard would mean another payment of sorts. A shake of your head, *I can't do that.*

Alighting at Lakemba station, Kevin leads the way, guiding you up Haldon Street. The houses are all similar, constructed of red brick, with overgrown grass and weed gardens, along with toys, broken furniture, and other rubbish strewn in the front yard. He points out landmarks, presuming that you might end up living here, though you're not convinced. Indicating a park with a rusting merry-go-round and a broken metal slide in the yellowing grass. 'People hang out here at night, but I'd avoid it.'

Your nerves tense, worried about getting your hopes up. Kevin, oblivious to your unease, continues acting as a tour guide. 'There's a Chinese takeaway on Canterbury Road,' he says, adding, 'It's a cheap place to eat.' He hesitates outside a fruit and veg corner shop and slips a green apple into his pocket. 'Watch out for the man inside. He'll rush out if he sees you.' He turns into a laneway alongside. Taking a large bite of the apple and beckoning you to follow him. 'C'mon. It's down here.'

At the end of the lane, he discards the apple core and points to a plain house across the street, resembling all the others with its red brick and low concrete front wall. The only distinguishing feature is a verandah with blue and white timber railings. On it sits a fifties-style lounge with rolled arms, its colour indistinguishable due to the layers of dirt covering it. He strides through the open front door, you follow, feeling a thrill of delight and an inexplicable sense of comfort as you enter. Over his shoulder, Kevin mouths, *it'll be alright*.

As you step into the hallway, you notice the worn-out carpet that covers the floor and the peeling floral wallpaper on the walls. Peeking through an open archway, you see a room with three iron beds and another room with more beds—further along the hallway, a door is fitted with a solid brass padlock. Kevin, noticing your glance, mutters, 'That's Betty and Steve's room. No one goes in there.' Reaching the end of the hallway, you recognise his cheeky grin as he casually opens a glass-panelled door and enters.

Inside, a massive rectangular table surrounded by mismatched timber chairs, one occupied by a boy. A large bay window offers a view of the unkempt rear garden. Facing a television, two faded brown material armchairs against a wall, another boy comfortably lounging in one of them, his arms adorned with blue-ink tattoos.

He turns to look at you, then turns away. The boy at the table shouts, 'Kevin's in trouble.'

'Hi Alfie.' Out of the side of his mouth, Kevin whispers, 'Don't worry about Alfie, he always shouts.'

'Kevin's in trouble,' Alfie repeated in a loud voice.

The aroma of frying onions fills the air, reminding you that it's been a while since you've eaten. There's a clatter of dishes and cursing from what you assume is the kitchen. The doorway has a set of multi coloured plastic strips above it. 'Hi Betty,' he yells, pushing them aside to let you enter; they slither and hiss back into place.

A woman in a faded house coat, with a yellow terry towelling cloth wrapped around her head, faces the stove, flour-covered hands on her hips. She turns around, sweat rolling down her face, grimacing. 'You're back then.'

'Yes, and I found Graham, the friend I told you about.'

She brushes a wisp of hair from her forehead, leaving a smudge of flour. 'Nice to meet you, Graham.' She beckons for you to come closer. Her eyes soften, and her mouth crinkles into a smile. 'So, you want to move in?'

Kevin grins. 'He does.'

Betty sniffs. 'Thank you, Kevin. Graham can answer for himself. Do your parents know where you are?'

Nodding, 'Yes, they, they're okay.' You recount the trip, leaving out a few things that she might not like to hear.

Her eyes remain focused on you, then, with a sigh, she turns back to the stove and lifts the frying pan of the burner. 'Let's try it for two weeks. Rent's thirty-five dollars a week ... in advance. I provide breakfast and dinner on weekdays, and breakfast and lunch on weekends. No smoking in the house, or swearing or fighting. You got the rent?'

Hesitating, remembering Kevin's words, 'Uh, a friend has promised to give me the money. I'm gonna get it.'

'I'm going with him,' Kevin adds.

'That'll help,' she says, with no hint of a smile. 'I've got one bed available. It's yours if you come back with the money by tomorrow.'

'I will, I will.' But, you're not so sure.

Kevin practices more of his tour guide expertise on the way out of the house. 'That's your bed,' pointing to one near the entrance to the second room. 'Mine's at the foot of yours. George sleeps around the corner. You'll meet him and the others later.'

If Reg gives me the money. 'We better go find Reg.'

Kevin nods. 'Yeah. Okay.'

≠

Back on a train, for the second time in two hours. You're intrigued by the older boy with the tattoos. You press Kevin about him. 'Who is he? He looks scary.'

'Neal? Nah. He's great. He's the only one with a single room, it's off the dining room. He's a friend of Betty's husband, Steve, both are from New Zealand.'

'Who else lives there?'

'You met Alfie. You can't talk to him; he only mutters or yells. Terry, he's the one who told me about the place.' He paused as the train rattled and swayed from side to side. 'Terry's family lives in Greenacre, but they don't want to see him. Betty has a soft spot for him, though. Peter, he's crippled, hurt in an accident, he doesn't say much, and Des, watch out for Des, he can be a bastard. The other boy I told you about, sleeps in our room, that's George. He's Greek, difficult to understand sometimes, but he's okay. Walks around a lot without his shirt on, flexing his muscles.' He goes quiet and looks out of the window.

'Is something wrong?'

'See those chimneys? I think that's the brewery. C'mon, here's the station.'

Redfern station's atmosphere is different from Lakemba. People jostle each other as they disembark from the train and rush through the turnstiles. The ticket collector ignores most of them, not asking for tickets, which is fortunate, as you don't have one. Kevin strides ahead, appearing sure of where he's going, moving past a group of terrace houses, their windows boarded up. You can't see anything that resembles a brewery, but Kevin forges on.

Children play in the alleyways, a football danced through the air, accompanied by laughter. One group of children, no older than five or six, propel a three-wheeled cart, squealing in delight as it splashes through the puddles.

Taking hold of his elbow. 'Should we be here?' Shrugging you off, he keeps walking. Staying close to him, then suddenly finding yourself too close as he comes to a halt and you walk smack-bang into him. 'Ouch.' Rubbing your nose, 'How about telling me when you're gonna stop.'

'This is it.'

'You sure?' Kevin nods.

The hotel sits on the corner of Redfern and Regent Streets. It may have been beautiful once, but now the green and white tiles on the walls are cracked and covered in dust and dirt. 'Bellevue Hotel' written on a sign on the wall.

'Where do we go? It's so fuckin' big.'

He points to a glass door with 'Public Bar' etched into it.

Hesitating, 'Can we go in?'

Lifting his shoulders, a brief look of annoyance on his face, 'If you wanna find this Reg, you have to. Anyway, we're here now.'

Shaking your head, 'I don't know if I can ask him for the money.'

'Shit. He said he'd help, didn't he?'

'People say lots of stuff.' You wipe your palms down the front of your jeans. Then, summoning up your courage, heart in mouth, you enter.

Two men glance in your direction and then return to their beers, each take a mouthful. The floor is sticky underfoot, like walking on flypaper, and there's an acrid smell of stale beer that makes your nose twitch. The barman, a glass in one enormous paw, looks at you.

Kevin whispers, 'Do you see him?' A shake of your head. 'Ask the barman. If he's a regular, he'll know him.'

The idea of approaching the stout-looking barman, with displeasure written all over his face, doesn't fill you with joy. Conscious of how you must look, long hair, torn jeans, you shuffle to the bar. Before you can open your mouth, he snaps, 'You kids shouldn't be in here. What do you want? C'mon, quick. I'll get in trouble if the boss sees you.'

'We're looking for someone. He drinks here. His name's Reg.'

The barman puts the glass down on the bar with a thump. 'Yeah, there's a Reg that drinks here. Wadda you want with him?'

Your spirits lift. 'Has he been in today?' The barman remains silent, still eyeing you suspiciously, waiting for more. 'We met him after he'd been to a rodeo.'

He relaxed, the beginnings of a smirk. 'Reg does love his rodeos.' Looking up at the clock, 'It's only two, and the brewery fellas knock off at four.' Grinning, 'He'll arrive five minutes later.'

A man seated on a stool in the corner swivels to face you. 'Reg tole me last night he'd got sum overtime. He'll be late.'

'Can I leave a message?'

'Ey what?' the barman asks.

'A message, can I leave one?'

He nods, handing you a crumpled, beer-stained docket, and a pencil, its end chewed to bare lead. Scribbling the message, you hand it back, he folds it and puts it in the till.

'You'll give it to him?'

'Yep. Now get outta here.'

Back on the street, turning to Kevin, 'What now?'

He has that impish grin again. 'I know a place where you can make money, if you're not too worried about what you do.'

Not knowing what he means, but a cold tremor suggests you might not like what he's got in mind. 'Where?'

'Not far. Easy money if you ...'

Annoyed, 'If you what?'

Sniggering, 'C'mon. I'll show you.' Playfully pinching your arm, amusement sparkled in his eyes. 'It's called the Wall.'

≠

He tells you about the Wall, at least what he knows, as you walk from the Bellevue. The more you hear, the less you want to go. Kevin stops.

'Is this it, the Wall? Doesn't look like what you said.'

Shaking his head, he points across the road. 'It's over there.' His breath rasps in his chest.

'You okay?'

'I ...' He gasps, takes a deep breath. 'I'm okay.' He gives you a weak smile. 'It comes and goes.'

'Why are we here?'

'Money.'

As you cross the street, your mind lingers on his words and the stories of those before you, driven by similar reasons. Your fingers trace the rough surface of the sandstone, contemplating the sweat and curses of the convicts who laid these massive blocks, each with their own marks and grooves—dates and fragments of names. *What would they say if they knew what this place had become?* The vision of scared and desperate boys, willing to do anything for a few pennies appears in your mind, startled, you pull your hand away abruptly. *Fuck, am I gonna do it too?*

Pushing the thought aside, you turn a corner, half-expecting to encounter a line of men clutching dollar notes in their hands. However, the sight surprises you: the wall is covered with drawings of impressive-sized cocks, phone numbers, and the names of meeting spots.

At the far end, a young boy leans against the corner. Noticing you, he tenses. His lank, straw coloured hair falls over his face, wafer thin legs protrude from baggy shorts held together by a makeshift rope belt. He glances once more before hurrying away. Shaken, you return to Kevin. 'We should leave.'

'Don't you wanna to make money?'

Letting out a long sigh, closing your eyes, unable to answer. *At what cost?* Hands shaking, you dig for the packet of Champion in your pocket. You'd snagged it from a man's coat, when he hung it on a hook in the toilets at the station. The packet jutted out of the top pocket, asking to be taken, too much to resist. Trembling, your fingers unable to roll the cigarette, tobacco spilling onto the pavement.

Kevin scoffs. 'You're making a mess of that. It's all over the fuckin' place.'

'Fuck off.' You look down, strands of tobacco litter the area around your feet. Sighing, you put the papers away and begin to tuck the Champion packet in your pocket.

'Pass it here. My dad smoked rollies, loved his Drum, and he showed me how to roll, when Mum wasn't looking.' A wistful look crosses his face, then disappears. 'Here.'

You light up and inhale, calming yourself. *Can I do this? If Reg doesn't give me the money, what choice do I have?* As if on cue, a car pulls up at the curb, the driver sits motionless, staring straight ahead. Whispering to Kevin, 'What's he waiting for?'

He grins. 'You'll see.'

'What?'

'Shhh.'

'Have you ever ...?'

Kevin hesitated, his eyes firmly fixed on the car and its occupant. 'Yeah, I let an old fart suck me off once. He gave me ten bucks. Cheap bastard.'

The driver crooked a finger in your direction. Kevin elbows you in the ribs. 'Go and see what he wants.'

Shaking your head, 'This is stupid.'

Another strike to your ribs. 'Go on.'

'Stop fucking doing that.'

'Do you want money or not?'

Grinding what's left of the soggy cigarette into the pavement, blanching, you walk towards the car, a sour taste in your mouth. A foot from the open window, your nostrils pick up the scent of Brut and sweat. The man leans across, his hand covered in coarse black hair. With a shudder, you've seen hands like that before.

≠

He lived in a flat two doors from your family in Windhoek. Whenever you went outside to play with your toy cars, he would appear at the railing one step above you, silently observing. He had a habit of always wearing a faded red flannelette dressing gown. Although he never spoke, his intense stare was unsettling. After a while, his dressing gown would open, revealing thick, white legs adorned with prominent blue veins and a limp cock. Without shifting his gaze, his hand, covered in a mass of black, curly hair, groped at himself, sliding up and down until he got an erection. As he stroked, he kept his eyes fixed on you, his breath becoming more ragged as the minutes passed. Then, he'd hastily retreat into his flat, slamming the door behind him.

On one occasion, his wife invited you to come inside and have a slice of cake. The temptation of the cake was hard to refuse, but you declined.

≠

'How, how much?' the man croaked, sweat on his brow, pants unzipped, the tip of a pasty cock poking out.

Unable to control the trembling, stuttering, 'F-f-for what?'

He takes his cock in his hand. 'To suck me off.'

Shaking your head, 'I don't. I can't.'

Baring his teeth, 'How much to suck you? Get in. I'll make it worth your while.'

'No ... I don't,' recoiling, tripping over your own feet, nearly landing flat on your back.

'You prick teaser. Fuck you,' he screams. The car roared away, tyres squealing, smoke belching from its exhaust as it veers into traffic. There's a cackle and snorting behind you. Over your shoulder you see Kevin clutching his belly, face contorted in glee.

'What's so fucking funny?'

'You,' he gurgles. 'I've never seen anyone move backwards that fast.' He performs an impression of you tripping over your own feet.

'Fuck off. I'm never coming back here.'

Breaking into another fit of giggles, dropping to his knees, Kevin pleads for you to stop. Clenching your hands, you step towards him. Taking a deep breath, he gets himself under control and glances at your hands, raising his own palms. 'Okay, okay.'

Chest heaving, you want to inflict pain on him, but stop yourself. 'What now?'

He wipes the tears from his eyes. 'Kings Cross isn't far. Do you wanna go there? Unless you want to try again?'

Furious, you walk away. The smile is gone as he joins you. 'C'mon, I'm only kidding. Also, you're going the wrong way.'

Your anger isn't directed at him but at yourself, ashamed at what you might have to do. You don't want to return to Darwin. *But does it mean I have to come back here?*

Kevin heads along Darlinghurst Road while you keep your distance—*Let him think I'm angry with him.* In fact, you're excited to be going to Kings Cross. You've seen the images of the gritty underworld. You envision gangsters and prostitutes hidden in the shadows of dark alleyways. However, that soon gives way to disappointment as reality proves different.

Rather than shady characters, the streets are bustling with people who resemble office workers more than anything else. They carry briefcases instead of guns or drugs, some dressed in safari suits, like your dad's. Young girls in mini-skirts and midriff tops mince along the pavement, mingling with elegant middle-aged ladies carrying designer bags labelled Gucci and Yves Saint Laurent. Despite the presence of strip clubs nestled between banks and butchers, everyone appears to be focused on their own business, paying no attention to them.

A boy thrusts a copy of the Daily Mirror in your hands, insisting you pay for it. 'It's yours,' he yells. Waving him away, laughing that he thinks you have money to waste. You see a man in brown velvet bell bottoms and a matching vest over a white T-shirt. His wide-brimmed hat, positioned at an angle, exudes an air of refinement, envy in your heart.

Kevin, meanwhile, is gawking at pictures of girls near the entrance to something called 'Pink Panther'. He squints, shading his eyes from the sun, whispering, 'Think we can get in?'

Oh no, not again, remembering the alleyway. You point to the bouncer at the entrance. 'That man, he's bigger than that bastard at the other place, where I might point out we nearly got killed.' Kevin chuckled, not a sound that fills you with hope that he'll take any notice.

The bouncer calls out to passers-by: 'Come in. Come in. Best girls in Sydney. The show's about to begin.' Most avert their gaze and hurry past. Then he glances at Kevin, who's still gawping at the pictures. 'Move along kid. Come back when you've got hair around your balls.' The man's stomach strains against his black frilled shirt, two buttons have popped open, rolls of neck fat over his collar. 'Go on, fuck off,' he mutters under his breath.

With a firm grip on Kevin's arm, you drag him away—you've had enough of angry men. A girl with thick black eyeshadow and glossy pink lips smiles at you. 'Don't worry about him boys, he's a shithead.' She wipes her hands down her arms, brushing away some imagined problem. With a cackle, 'If you boys want fun, come back and see me?' Rushing past, she screeches at our retreating backs, 'I'll do both of you.' You've found the Kings Cross you expected. Kevin's breathing is ragged again. You help him sit on a bench, worried he might collapse as a cough racks his chest. 'Will you be okay?' He nods.

Moving away, but keeping one eye on him, you roll a cigarette. The smoke catches in your throat and you start coughing. You hear Kevin muttering that you sound like him. Throwing the smoke away, now mostly soggy paper, you're still unable to roll a decent cigarette. 'What now?'

'There's a shop not far from here,' he wheezes. 'The lady who runs it is nice. We can hang out there for a while.'

You help him up. 'We can't be too long. I don't wanna miss Reg.'

'You won't. C'mon.' He looks to be improving as you cross the road, his breathing under control. The area is different here. Out of sight of the public, the buildings are dirtier, rubbish piled up on the pavement.

Two girls in a doorway look in your direction. They exchange nods, and one takes a step towards you. 'Got a light, luv?' A gold mini-skirt highlights slender legs, red blotches on her knees. Thick make-up can't cover her pockmarked face. With a whine, 'Well, got a light for a girl or not?' You fumble for your matches, a cloying, sweet perfume engulfs you as she moves closer. You offer the matches; she takes them with a sharp movement. Strikes a match, lights her cigarette, sucks in a lungful of smoke, then tucks the matchbox between her breasts. 'Thanks, luv. Are youse looking for something special?' She winks and looks over her shoulder at her friend. Bending forward, her breasts try to free themselves from her top, she hoots, 'We'll give you a reel good time, both of you.' When you don't accept her offer, she glances at Kevin, and then, with a sniff, turns and walks back to her friend, hips swaying from side to side.

Kevin leads you to a quaint shop filled with spinning wind chimes, and racks of cheesecloth shirts and dresses. When you enter, a bell tinkles, announcing your arrival. A lady behind the counter claps her hands when she spots Kevin. He leans toward you and whispers. 'This woman is a gypsy, so behave.'

'Me? Fuck you.'

She hurries over and embraces him. 'Lovely to see you again. Are you looking for another hat?' She twitters, 'Who's your friend?'

'This is Graham. I was wondering if we can sit at the back. We're waiting to meet someone.'

Her eyes sparkle. 'I hope it's someone nice.' Smiling, 'Of course. I do have a client, but I'm sure he won't mind. Would you like some water?' You both nod.

Kevin plonks himself onto a large cushion in front of a curtained booth. You drop into a beanbag; it squeaks each time you adjust your position. *You'd like to meet whoever invented these fuckin things.*

As you sit there, a man hurries past, his actions furtive as he enters the booth. Sensing your curiosity, the lady deliberately leaves the curtain open as she sits and shuffles a deck of cards. She then begins a hushed conversation with the man, who listens intently and responds with a smile.

Kevin's snoring and restless tossing distracts you from the problem on your mind. *Will Reg lend it to me?* Poking Kevin to wake him up, he stirs, blinks sleepily like an owl. 'Huh, what? What's up?'

'We should go and find Reg?'

'Uh, yeah, um, okay, give me a minute.' He snuggles back into the cushion.

In exasperation, you kick his leg. 'For fuck's sake. C'mon.' He groans and pushes himself up off the cushion.

Heading back to the Bellevue, anxious and nervous, your mind filled with doubt. *What if he's not there, or worse, unwilling to help?* The confidence you had earlier begins to wane as you face the moment of truth, fingernails gnawed away by the time you arrive.

You hesitate. Kevin groans. 'What's wrong now?'

'I don't ... What if he can't? If he doesn't lend me the money?'

Kevin puts an arm around your shoulders. 'If he's not here, then we'll go back to the Wall together and make the money.'

'You'd ... you'd really do that ... for me?'

'Shit yeah.'

Taking a deep breath, you know you have to find out, and buoyed by his words you enter the pub. The same two men are at their table, nursing beers. The only other occupants are another man and a woman, deep in conversation. But no Reg. And a different barman behind the bar wiping down the top. Looking up, he scowls. 'Kids aren't allowed in here.'

You open your mouth to ask about Reg, but it snaps shut as he strolls into the bar through a door marked 'Toilet' and breaks into a smile. 'Graham, good to see you again,' wrapping his brawny arms around you. He hasn't changed a bit, the sweat-stained akubra still jammed on his head. 'I got your note. Plenty of beer here, so I didn't mind waiting. Who's your friend?' You introduce Kevin. 'Would you like a drink? Lemon squashes?'

Kevin leans across. 'We have to be quick or we won't get back in time for dinner.'

'Now we have to be quick? Geez, he's lending me money.'

Reg returns with four drinks on a tray, two of them beers. 'Cheers,' he says, taking a gulp. 'Ah, that's good.' Reaching into his pocket, he pulls out an envelope and slides it across the table. 'Here you go.'

'I ... don't. Thank you. I'll pay it back. I promise.'

He nods. 'I know you will, or I wouldn't give it to you. There's a bit extra in there to tide you over.' The envelope is thick and heavy in your hands. You want to open it right away but resist the urge. *When I'm on the train.*

Kevin puts down his empty glass and begins fidgeting in his seat, his breathing shallow. He quickly huffs, 'We better go.'

Reg chuckles. 'Where's this place?'

'It's in Lakemba. I guess we had better go.' There's a tear in the corner of your eye as you stand and say goodbye. With a sniff, 'I ...' struggling to find the words.

Reg waves you to silence. 'You helped me out. I'm glad I can return the favour. Funny how these things work out.' Shaking hands, promising again that you'll pay him back as soon as you can.

≠

There's no tour this time as Kevin hurries out of Lakemba station, like a starving man rushing to a banquet. 'Betty's strict about meal times. She shuts the kitchen if you're late.' He says, puffing.

You arrive to find Betty hovering over the stove. Wiping her brow, she beams at Kevin. 'I didn't think you'd miss dinner.' Glancing at you, 'Does this mean you're moving in Graham?'

Nodding like an excited puppy, 'Yes, yes, I am,' handing her the money. She stuffs it down the front of her housecoat.

'Kevin, show Graham where he'll be sleeping. Dinner will be ready soon. Alfie, come and help set the table.'

Kevin takes the bag off your shoulder, and with a grin that's a mile wide, escorts you to the bed he showed you a few hours ago. He shouts, 'George, we've got a new roommate.'

A bare-chested boy, a blue singlet over his shoulder, stomps around the corner. 'This your friend?' He has long, curly brown hair, which he sweeps back from his face with one hand. Grinning, 'Hope you don't mind noise. Kevin snores all night.'

Kevin's smile fades. 'Shut up. I don't.'

'If it's not snoring, then it must be farting,' George says, smirking.

You enjoy the joking between them, but the reality is you don't know how long you can stay. With a sigh, you mutter, 'I gotta find a job.'

'Betty said something about that. Ask her. She'll take care of you.' George walks back around the corner.

Kevin introduces the others at dinner, a series of nods around the table, except for Des, his eyes hooded as he studies you, impossible to tell what he's thinking.

Betty, with a bowl of steaming mashed potato in one hand, leans over your shoulder. 'The boys are going to a dance tonight. Why don't you go?'

Terry, putting his knife and fork down, 'Yeah, you should. There'll be lots of girls.'

'Girls, girls,' Alfie chants.

'Alfie, be quiet,' George says, ladling mash onto his plate. Terry grins at you. 'You wanna come?'

Neal's eyes narrow. 'Be careful. There are Sharpies at those dances and they don't like long hairs.' Terry, George and Kevin all nod in agreement.

It's when you're on the train, heading to the dance, that you decide to find out what Neal meant. 'Are they the same Sharpies as at the snooker place?'

He laughs and looks at Terry. 'You know more about Sharpies than me. Tell Graham about 'em.' Terry ignores him, which only makes him more insistent. 'C'mon, tell him.'

Terry, frowning, turns and stares at you. 'You wanna know?' You nod. Sighing, he glances out the window. 'All you need to know is to stay away from them.'

'Why don't they like long hair?'

He looks daggers at you. 'They don't need a reason. They hate blond-haired surfies as well, a bit like you Kevin.' He sniffs. 'But everyone's fair game.' Then, with a shake of his head, he mutters, 'Make sure you don't go near their brushs.'

'They carry brushes?'

Terry studies you as if you're making fun of him, and decides you're not. 'Brushs are their chicks. They belong to 'em. Now shut up, we're nearly there.'

Terry guides us along Beamish Street. Kevin insists, we take a shortcut through a park, but Terry shakes his head. 'It's not a good idea.' Kevin is about to argue, until a look from George makes him decide otherwise. You feel a sense of contentment being with Terry, George and Kevin. Like family.

Kevin grasps Terry's arm, to hurry him up. Grumbling, he shoves him away. 'What the fuck? What's your hurry?'

'I don't wanna miss any of the fun.' Then, seeing the long line to get into the hall, Kevin moans, 'I told you.'

Entering the crowded hall, you struggle through the mass of bodies to find an unoccupied part of the wall to watch the action. The dance floor is alive with a sea of people, moving together to the beat under the glow of pulsating lights. Kevin decides to explore, leaving you alone with Terry. George disappeared the moment we stepped inside.

He elbows you. Wincing, you turn to him, as he points at a group of boys in a corner, dancing in a wild and chaotic manner that resembles a fight more than a dance. One of them, who appears to be their leader, is wearing sailor pants with braces over a buttoned, up polo shirt. Terry whispers, 'See' em?' You nod. 'I know one. Stay well clear.' *Why would I go near them?*

You focus back on the girls on the dance floor, concerned by Kevin's absence.

You scan the crowd, but there's no sign of him. You worry that he might have found himself in trouble again. When you least expect it, Kevin appears beside you, catching you off guard. 'This dance is stupid. Do you wanna leave?'

Tugging on Terry's shirtsleeve, 'You coming?' He shakes his head. George is nowhere to be seen, but he can look after himself. Mouthing *See you at home*, you like saying *home*. You don't notice that the Sharpies are no longer in the corner. Outside, punching Kevin on the shoulder, you laugh. 'I didn't meet any girls. What about you?'

He mutters, 'I didn't like any of them.'

'Bullshit, you like 'em all. They don't like you.'

Arm around your neck, he shouts, 'Fuck off. I could if I wanted.' The two of you wrestle each other like two drunks, yelling and laughing at the top of your voices, staggering from side to side across the road. Panting, Kevin stops. 'C'mon, we can cut through the park. It'll save time.'

Getting your breath back, shaking your head, 'Terry didn't think it was a good idea.'

'Fuck him. He's not here.'

Staring at the paved entrance to the park, looking into the inky blackness, you tend to agree with Terry. 'Are you sure about this?'

'Don't be chicken. It's okay.'

With a determined air, he starts along the path, and, as is becoming your habit, you follow. The glow from the streetlights begins to fade, a noise in the bushes raises the hair on the back of your neck. Grasping his shoulder, 'I think we should go back.' Then, a crunch from behind, faint but you heard it. Swivelling around, nothing. Moving alongside Kevin, 'Did you hear that?'

You can't see his face but there's scorn in his voice. 'For fuck's sake, get a grip. C'mon, it's not far.'

A piercing whistle rips through the night. You freeze, unsure of what's happening. 'Kevin, what … what the fuck was that?'

He looks left and then right, voice wavering. 'I, I don't, I can't …'

Peering into the dark, you can't see anything either. Catching his arm, 'Should, should we keep going?' Another whistle, louder and closer.

'Shit!' Kevin exclaims.

Glancing in the same direction he's looking, your heart races so fast that you feel a sharp pain in your chest. Through the shadows, you make out the figure of the Sharpie in sailor pants, he stands in the middle of the path. Raising a hand to his lips he lets out a short, sharp whistle. From the surrounding trees, leaves rustle, and branches crack as Sharpies drop one by one to the ground.

Kevin screams, 'Run, run, for fuck's sake, run!'

You hurdle through the thick bushes, ignoring the stinging branches, desperately trying to outrun the sharpie in sailor pants. Frustrated, he yells, 'Get the cunts. Get 'em.' There's a thud and a moan behind you. Fear seizes you as you focus on escaping rather than looking behind. Kevin is ahead, shouting something, but you can't understand him. Your lungs burn with each breath.

Finally, you burst out of the park onto an empty street, bathed in the weak glow of a solitary street light. Relief washes over you spotting the railway station.

A panicked scream from Kevin. 'Fuck, the train is arriving. Shit, shit, we're gonna miss it.'

Summoning the last ounce of strength, you both sprint towards the station. The Sharpies seem to have vanished, but you can't shake the feeling that they're close. With Kevin's frantic screams urging you on, you hurdle the turnstile, stumbling and falling to one knee. *Where the fuck are they?*

'Get up, get up. They're coming,' Kevin screams from an open carriage door. The Sharpie in sailor pants attempts to jump the turnstile, his trousers snag, and he tumbles to the ground.

Kevin screams again, 'Hurry, hurry.' Launching yourself across the platform, you dive headfirst into the carriage as the train begins to pick up speed, moving out of the station. Looking back, the Sharpies surround the boy in sailor pants still lying on the ground. One stares at you menacingly, making a threatening gesture across his throat. Now on the moving train, full of bravado. Both you and Kevin respond with raised fingers.

Kevin wipes the sweat from his face, but he's smiling, as if it's all a game. Shivering, you think about the mayhem that would have occurred if they'd made it onto the train. *I'm not gonna tell him how scared I am.* Knees pulled up to your chest, arms around them, you hope this is your only encounter with Sharpies. If only you could see into the future.

≠

Startled, you wake from a dream. Sharpies are pulling you off a train, kicking and stomping. A glance around the room reassures you, it's in your mind. With relief, you wait for the trembling to subside. Your thoughts shift to the job that Betty's arranging. Anxiety creeps in. *What if I mess it up?*

Slipping out of bed, treading quietly to the dining room, feeling an unexplainable chill even though the evening is warm. The round moon casts long shadows, adding to your unease. Something about the moon tugs at the edges of your memory, but its grasp eludes you. Turning to head back to bed, you halt. Neal stands in front of his bedroom door, arms folded across his chest—a scraping accompanied by a fleeting shadow behind the door.

Did I imagine that? Must have. We're not allowed.

Flexing his fingers, stepping towards you, he hisses, 'Why are you creeping around the house at night?'

'I'm, I'm not. I couldn't sleep.'

'You up to summit?'

'No. The job, I ... '

With a slow smile, he relaxes. 'Betty doesn't like anyone wandering around the house at night. Betta get to bed.'

'Sure, sure.' You glance again at the door, the light under it a solid beam. *I must have imagined it.* Neal's eyes bore into you as you leave.

The morning after the dance, Betty tapped you on the shoulder. 'I've got good news. A friend of mine needs an extra pair of hands at his factory, you can start Monday. It's near Punchbowl Road, so you'll have to catch a bus. Steve can show you. He goes that way.'

'I ... I ... uh ... I don't know what to say.' She smiles, fiddling with the scarf around her head. Kevin winks.

'Catch the number six. Got it?' Steve says, you nod. 'It's the same bus back.' Looking you in the eye, he adds,

'Betty's gone to a lot of trouble to arrange this. Do a good job. Ey?'

As the bus departs, you find yourself in a gritty, industrial area–with padlocked doors and barred windows. Wilson's Joinery is wedged between Johnson's Panel Beaters and an electronics shop that promises free installation for every Rank Arena television bought.

Pushing open a glass sliding door, you enter the joinery office. A girl behind a desk ignores you, engrossed in admiring her fingernails under the glow of a desk lamp.

'Hi. I'm, uh, I'm Graham. Here for, uh, Betty said ...'

Startled, quickly hiding her hand, she glares, irritated. 'What? Betty? Betty who?'

'She said she'd, uh, she'd arranged for ...'

'Oh. You're the kid dad mentioned this morning. He's not here. Eric's the foreman. He'll get you started.' With a forceful shove, her chair collides with the wall as she rises and strides towards a door labelled 'Staff Only.' As it swings open, hammering, drilling, and sawing greets you like a gut punch.

She gestures to a man in an animated discussion with two others. He flings the paper he's waving under their noses onto a bench before storming over, hands buried deep within his blue overalls. 'What? What do you want?'

The girl, visibly shaken by his abrupt manner, 'He's, dad said, he …' She nods at you. 'He's starting today.'

He sizes you up, then looks back at her. 'He didn't say nothing to me.'

'He's here.'

Fixing his eyes on you again, 'You can work this?' He waves a hand at the workshop. A shake of your head, causes him to mutter under his breath, and throw his hands in the air as he leaves.

One of the men who'd been in discussion with him wanders over with a friendly smile. Black spots cover his cheeks. 'Sharon, is everything okay?' Sighing, she repeats what she told the foreman.

He laughs. 'I'll take care of it.' Sticking out his hand, 'I'm Gary. What's yours?'

'Uh, Graham.'

'Don't worry about Eric. He gets cranky but he's okay most of the time. Let's kit you out and then get you started. There'll be overalls in the storeroom.' He looks you up and down. 'I reckon we'll have something that'll fit you. You'll need boots too.' You glance down—there's a hole in one shoe.

Exhaling, Sharon walks away, slamming the door behind her. Gary grins and leads you across the workshop, past benches stacked with furniture in various stages of assembly. Taking a deep breath, hesitating, Trevor in your head as Gary enters a storeroom. He looks over his shoulder. 'C'mon.' Palms sweating, stomach clenched, you step inside. Gary pulls a box off a shelf and digs through it, letting out a loud snort, he holds up a pair of overalls. 'Told ya. These'll work a charm. Get changed in the loo.' The overalls smell of sweat and sawdust, but they fit, as does the pair of old boots. 'Alright. Now, what can you do?'

'Um. I worked in a laundry.'

'Not much call for that here. Let's start you on something easy.' He takes you over to the buzz-saw. The man operating it watches as you approach and switches the machine off. Your ears continue to ring in the sudden silence. Placing his hands in the crook of his back he makes a show of stretching, a frown on his face. 'Brett, meet Graham, he's starting today. I'm gonna get him to carry the sawn timber to the benches, okay?' Brett grunts, turns away and starts up the saw. Hands over his ears, Gary yells, 'You'll get used to it.'

An hour passes, and the effort has taken a toll on your arms, leaving them numb. Fine sawdust has found its way into your nose and throat, making it difficult to breathe. A sharp whistle pierces the air, jolting you, dropping the timber, it clatters against your shins before crashing to the floor. Everyone disappears through a door at the back of the workshop.

Gary, laughing, helps you pick up the timber. 'That old bugger Eric should be happy. You've helped speed up the work. C'mon, smoko time.'

A blue cloud fills the room. Everyone is gathered around a table, holding cigarettes and enjoying their cuppa from steaming mugs. Gary gestured towards a kitchenette, 'Help yourself, Graham.'

A tin marked coffee rests beside a bubbling urn, there's an assortment of chipped cups on a timber shelf along with a plastic container labelled 'Sugar' in black biro.

The whistle sounds again, and all rise as one. Gary yells, 'Finish your coffee, Graham, then wash up,' before he leaves.

Within a few days, you feel at ease in the job and among the men. Unexpectedly, you find yourself designated as the cup washer following each break. After a week, Gary assigns you a new task—fixing cloth to the bases of lounge frames using a stapling gun. However, after accidentally stapling your fingers to the timber frames, twice, Gary suggests switching to gluing—much safer, he mutters.

As you leave for work on Friday morning, Betty, with a shout, reminds you that the rent is due, assuring her you won't forget, you hurry out of the house.

≠

Gary slaps you on the back, 'Pay time,' propelling you towards the queue outside the door to the front office. Sharon is there—it's the first time you've encountered her since you began.

In her hands, a stack of yellow envelopes and a sheet of paper. She called each person by name, and they collected their envelope and signed the sheet. When it's your turn, you take your envelope. By chance, your fingers lightly brush against hers. She's oblivious to the brief touch and motions for you to sign with a tap of her red fingernail.

Gary puts an arm around your shoulders. 'Hey, we're heading to the pub. Are you coming?' Knowing you had to get back and pay the rent, you hesitate, about to refuse, changing your mind when he turns to Sharon. 'How about you Shaz?'

She nods. 'Yep.'

Rent forgotten, 'I'll come.'

Of all of the men, Gavin is the closest in age to you. During the night, he and Sharon spend their time whispering to each other, not once glancing in your direction. Eventually, Gavin proposes that everyone continue the evening playing cards and drinking at his flat, and you have an idea why.

You lie on the lounge, stealing occasional glances at Sharon, admiring her figure in her jeans and knitted top. Filled with thoughts of her, you drift off to sleep.

You wake, sitting upright wide-eyed. *Where am I?* Then, you remember Sharon and the events from the night. Everything is eerily quiet, and the room is empty, and no Sharon. Panic sets in as you spot the clock showing it's already seven in the morning. Your thoughts turn to Betty. *Fuck, rent.*

With your stomach in knots, you rush to catch the bus and sprint as fast as you can from Lakemba bus stop to the front door. Making your way down the hallway and into the dining room, Kevin and Terry are finishing breakfast. They both grin at the expression on your face. Kevin sniggers, 'You're in trouble.'

'Fuck. What, what did ...?'

'Betty took your stuff and locked it in her room.'

'Shit. What ...?'

Kevin, looking thoughtful, not easy for him, suggests, 'Hide in the kitchen and then jump out and surprise her.'

In a low voice, Terry says, 'She's coming.'

You can't think of anything else to do, so you duck into the kitchen, Kevin, always ready to do something silly, joins you.

'You finished?' Betty says to Terry, marching through the doorway.

With a mouthful of cornflakes, he mumbles, 'Nearly.'

'Good.' She strides into the kitchen without glancing left or right.

'Hey Betty!' Kevin shouts, 'Look who I found.'

Betty jumps, pressing her hands against her chest. 'Kevin, don't, you'll give ...' She stops, her lips forming a thin line. 'Graham. What did I say about rent being due on Fridays?'

Your heart sinks as you fight back tears. 'Sorry. They all went for a drink and I lost track of time. I, I'm ...'

A smile tugs at the corners of her mouth, eyes twinkling, 'Steve reckoned that's what happened. I'm gonna have a word with that boss of yours, taking a young 'un to the pub. I put your stuff in my room for safekeeping.'

'It won't happen again, I promise.' Pulling the rent money out of your pocket, and handing it over. Betty stuffs it down the front of her top; you're sure no-one will get their hands on it now.

'Everyone can make a mistake. Want some breakfast?'

'Yes please.' Kevin and Terry smile as Betty places an empty bowl on the table, squeezing your shoulder.

≠

'I'm bored,' Kevin announces, making himself comfortable on your bed. Terry, in his usual don't-give-a-shit way, tells him to get off his arse and do something about it then. Kevin, ignoring him, 'How about we go to Luna Park?'

You don't know what Luna Park is, and after the various events that Kevin has led you into, you're wary. 'What's Luna Park?'

Terry pipes up. 'It's great. It's got dodgems, a roller-coaster, and girls.'

It was a familiar story with him—always 'girls', but you never met any. Still, one day that might change, shrugging, 'If you wanna.'

Terry shuffles from foot to foot, obviously wanting to say something more. You think it might be about Kevin, but instead, says, 'Umm, I got a friend who lives close. We can crash there, after, if you want to.'

Kevin hops off your bed. 'Great, let me get my hat.' He starts rummaging through the wardrobe.

Terry rolls his eyes. 'Oh, for fuck's sake.'

You hear Kevin mumble indistinctly, then he turns around, top hat in hand. 'Girls love it, you'll see.' Walking away, Terry mutters that Kevin never meets girls, so how the fuck would he know?

At the mention of dodgems, a rush of nostalgia washes over you to a day at Blackpool Pier. You can almost taste it—the sweetness of sticky pink fairy floss on your lips, and the striped rock candy. As the day stretched on, so did the candy.

The arcades are alive with flashing lights and a kaleidoscope of colours. Tinkling bells and triumphant whistles in the air—the carnival games calling you to spend your precious few pennies.

Amidst this, your mother, eyes ablaze with the thrill of playing her favourite game, Bingo. You smile, remembering her expression as the caller announced each number, followed by a gasp if she won. The memory of your father is different. His presence is a silhouette, as if he were a shadow, not really there.

$$\neq$$

'Can you believe the crowd here?' Kevin shouts, his eyes wide with wonder. You scan the bustling scene, taking in the mix of people as you enter through a smiling clown's mouth, the air thick with anticipation, finding yourself torn between apprehension and the irresistible pull of excitement.

Luna Park casts a spell, and you're instantly captivated by what lies before you. The scent of popcorn and fairy floss fills the air, mingling with the distant sound of laughter and screams from those on the rides.

A wooden roller-coaster, an old relic, creaks and groans as it climbs up a steep incline. The sheer excitement and terror of those on-board echoes in their shouts. On the Ferris wheel, boys swing their legs and sway the carriages, their laughter carrying clearly across the park. A stilt-walking man dressed in a glimmering silver suit stands out. He drops a flyer into your hand with a flourish. Terry nudges Kevin towards the ticket booth. 'Get the tickets, hey? Then we can go on the Mouse.' You catch Kevin's eye and silently exchange a question: *What's the Mouse?*

As he stands in line to purchase tickets, you study the people flocking through the entrance—or, more precisely, the girls. Terry draws your attention to two. He whispers, eyes alight, 'I saw them look at us when we came in. We should say hello.'

Shocked, you shake your head. 'I can't walk up and ...'

'Why not?'

The girls have their tickets and are heading for the Ferris wheel as Kevin comes hurrying back. A sudden gust of wind whips the top hat off his head. 'Shit,' he yells, dodging between legs, trying to grab it. A slim foot in a tan sandal, stamps on the brim. 'Here,' the owner of the sandal says, picking it up and handing it back to him. He mutters from the side of his mouth. 'Told you.' You ignore him, realising the girl is one of those that Terry had pointed out earlier. Her bob hairstyle frames a round face and upturned nose. Her friend, the taller of the two, irritated by our interruption, crosses her arms over her chest.

Terry introduces himself, then Kevin, then you. 'Kevin's the stupid one,' he says. Annoyed, Kevin turns away.

'I'm Stacey, this is Deborah.'

Terry doesn't wait for any more pleasantries. 'Want to join us on the Wild Mouse? It's grouse.' Your stomach lurches at the thought of going on a roller-coaster.

Stacey, hesitating, 'Nah, we're gonna go on the Ferris wheel. We could ...' Deborah, pulling on her arm, drags her away before she can finish.

The three of you head for the pirate ship, then the dodgems. Kevin wants to go on Coney Island. You argue that it looks boring, Terry moans, 'It's rubbish,' but Kevin doesn't listen. He hurries up the path, disappearing inside. You both follow and get absorbed in the rotating barrels and Devil's drop. You piss yourselves at your reflections in the mirror maze, and flop like headless chickens on the crazy floor.

Your attention turns to finding Kevin. Eventually, discovering him at a photo booth, insisting on capturing a picture to commemorate the day's adventures. The booth features a mock jail cell, and the three of you pose behind bars. However, a shiver runs down your spine as you recall your recent encounter with the police, casting a shadow over you.

Terry takes the remaining tickets from Kevin. 'We only have enough for two more rides. And we haven't been on the bloody roller-coaster or Ghost train yet. They're the best. Let's ...' He spies Stacey munching on a battered sav, tomato sauce dripping down her fingers. Strolling over, 'Youse wanna go on the roller-coaster with us?'

'Oooh, I don't know, it looks scary.' She licks the last of the sauce from her fingers and looks at Deborah, who nods. Stacey grins at Terry, 'If you take care of us,' fluttering her eyelashes—not that she needs to.

Deborah's mouth gapes open, a silent scream frozen on her face as you rocket around the twisting track. The wind rushes past, tugging at the edges of her mouth. Her eyes are as wide as saucers. Terry, with arms raised above his head, fingers splayed, grasps at the rushing wind. You hang onto the safety bar. Knuckles pale against red metal as you plummet down a heart-stopping drop, a rush of blood surging through your veins. In the joy of being alongside a girl, you'd forgotten your fear of heights—it came back.

Deborah lets out a full-throated scream that echoes across Sydney Harbour. The roller coaster comes to a halt, its wheels screeching against the metal rails, your body trembles.

Deborah leans over to Stacey, her face a shade of white, stuttering, 'We, we gotta go.' Stacey doesn't reply.

Kevin waits patiently, having said no to going on the roller-coaster, claiming it makes his breathing difficult. Taking you aside, he says, 'I'm going to go home.'

'Why?'

'Stacey likes Terry, and I reckon you got a chance with Deborah.'

'Don't think so.' But as you watch him leave, part of you is glad, hoping you do have a chance with Deborah. He looks forlorn as he treks out of the park, red top hat in hand, and you feel a tremor of guilt.

Kevin had become a close friend with whom you shared countless weekends. The bond wasn't just about hanging out together but rather experiencing life. You'd stood side by side on a stormy night outside the Hordern Pavilion, the sound of rain blending with Jethro Tull.

You spent time in the Domain, with its sprawling green expanse. Speaker's Corner attracted you, not for the discussion but for the faint hope of encountering girls. Dressed in your hippie clothing, a sleeveless army jacket adorned with a peace sign painted in white on the back and jeans with a British flag patch, you appeared cool, or so you thought. The smiles and whispers from passing girls kept you hopeful—but the clothing may have been the reason you eventually didn't have any success.

Looking back, it's clear that time was more about being together, sharing friendship, although you didn't recognise it then, for what it was.

Deborah gives you a sidelong glance as Kevin leaves, and you promptly forget about him. Terry doesn't even notice, too busy talking to Stacey. 'Where's Kevin?' he finally asks.

'He's gone. Didn't wanna hang around. Reckons the girls aren't interested in him.'

'Of course not. It's that fuckin' hat. He looks stupid.'

Tired of his attitude, guilty about Kevin leaving, snapping, 'Fuck off. We wouldn't have met them if it hadn't been for the bloody hat.' Terry turns away as it begins to drizzle. The girls look miserable and cold.

Terry, arm around Stacey, wants one ride on the Ghost Train. 'After that, we can go see my friend. His place isn't far and it'll be warm.' The girls exchange glances, and then, to your surprise and delight, they agree. Terry and Stacey get in the front carriage, with Deborah and you behind. Ghoulish laughter comes from the tunnel as you enter.

Terry slides closer to Stacey, his arm firmly around her shoulders—it's still there when you burst out of the exit, laughing and yelling. Deborah slid close to you when a ghostly figure jumped out of the shadows, then moved away.

Outside, large drops of rain splash onto the ground, and a thunderclap makes you jump. Terry yells, 'Let's go.' With Stacey's hand in his, he runs through the park; you take Deborah's and follow. As they race up a set of steps, slippery from the rain, you and Deborah try to keep up, panting as you reach the top. They keep going, across a road and into a side street. Over his shoulder, Terry shouts, 'Nearly there.' Turning into a cobbled laneway, running single file until he stops in front of a weathered green door. The girls, breathing hard, lean against the wall, water dripping from their chins, Deborah's hair flattened on top of her head.

He bangs on the door. It opens to reveal a boy looking like he's just woken up. 'Shit, Terry, get outta this.' He moves out of the way as we hurry inside. The girls screw up their noses at the stink of unwashed clothing, but you're all glad to be out of the rain.

Terry introduces Evan, as his girlfriend wanders into the hallway to find out what all the noise is about. She's not impressed at having visitors. Evan, taking her hand,

'He's a friend … you know.' He introduces her as Zoe as he exchanges a look with Terry. 'Here, let's find dry clothes. There's T-shirts and other shit somewhere.' Evan disappears into an adjacent room, reappearing, arms laden with an assortment of clothing. Pointing towards the room he'd just left. 'Guys, change in there. The girls can use the bathroom.'

The dry clothes warm you from the chill that has seeped into your bones, even though they have an unpleasant smell. As if something had died in them. The girls, relax too.

Your gaze wanders around the room, taking in the boarded-up fireplace, a cracked and worn marble mantle wrapped around it. Your eyes turn to the four-poster bed, Zoe already under the blankets, the tip of her nose the only visible part.

Evan met your glance with a knowing expression. His lips curled into a half-smile. 'We stay in bed to keep warm. There's fuck all heating.' He continued, 'But I don't think we'll all fit. There's an old sofa bed in the other room. Terry and uh …?

''Stacey,' Terry says.

'Yeah, Terry and Stacey can crash here.'

Deborah sniffs the tracksuit she's got on and pauses. 'We don't know how long we're gonna stay. Stace, wadda ya think?'

The storm continues to rage, a timber window frame rattles, Stacey climbing into the bed, pauses, 'Um, let's stay until the rain stops.' Sliding under the blanket, pulling it up to her chin.

Seeing the concern in Deborah's eyes, you ask, 'Will anyone worry about you?'

Stacey, poking her nose over the top of the blanket, sniggered, 'Nah. I'm supposed to be at Deborah's, and she told her mum she's at my place, so no-one's expecting us home.'

Terry laughs. 'That's great.'

Deborah, shrugging, 'Looks like we're staying for a bit. Let's check out the other room.'

The sofa bed had seen better days, stuffing poked out of the cushions. Grabbing the base, you both tug until, with a loud screech, the bed collapses onto the floor. A grey woollen blanket showers you in dust. Ignoring the mess, climbing under the blanket, Deborah sneezes. 'I'm glad we're away from Evan. I get the creeps off him, and his girlfriend looks pissed off.'

You nod. 'Yeah. I think Terry and Evan were with a Sharpies gang. They're mates, but I know what you mean.'

Burrowing into the bed, you drift off to sleep, only waking when Deborah's arm flops across your chest. She's still fast asleep, so you slide out of bed to talk to Terry.

In the other room, Stacey is standing in the middle, face red, hands on her hips, hollering, 'I'm not like that.' Bemused, Terry is sitting up in bed. Evan and Zoe remain hidden under the bedclothes. Stacey turns to you, barking, 'Where's Deborah?'

'Uh, she's asleep. Why? What's up?

'We're leaving. Wake her.'

Hearing the commotion, Deborah, is sitting up in bed, a quizzical look on her face. 'What happened?'

'Stacey wants to leave. You gonna go?'

'She's my friend.'

Stacey stomps into the hallway. 'Deb, you ready? I wanna get out of here.'

Deborah, squeezing your hand. 'Thanks. I gotta go.'

You want to say you'd like to see her again, but she's gone. Kicking yourself. *Will I ever find a girl?*

≠

The tension is physical as you sit alongside Terry on the weathered verandah, hanging like an unspoken question. His voice, usually composed, carries a quiver, a sign he's grappling with something. You strain to catch each word, trying to piece together what's happening. Worry is etched on his features.

There's a rawness to his voice that strikes a chord deep within you. 'I need to leave.'

'Why?'

Hanging his head, 'I don't ... I can't stay.'

'Where are you gonna go?'

'Back to the boys.'

'Do you mean the Sharpies?' He stares at the ground. 'Shit, you'll end up ....'

The tension dials up as Des walks out of the front door, squaring his shoulders, his face twisting into a sneer. 'What are you two bludgers up to?'

You've learnt the lesson of hiding yourself to make sure you're not noticed. It's a survival technique, one well-honed from previous experience. But tonight is not one of those times. 'Why don't you fuck off?'

His eyes glitter, an inexplicable hate in them. He flexes his fists, scowling, 'You wanna go, do ya?'

Getting to your feet, shouting, 'Fuck you.'

'You haven't got the guts.' He taunts.

Terry grabs your arm. 'Leave it. Remember Betty's rules?'

Shaking his hand off, a white-hot rage burns in your gut, 'Fuck that. He's been pushing ever since I got here.'

Des strides into the front garden and you follow, the anger bubbling up, years in the making. Raising your hands, you throw a wild haymaker that connects with nothing but air. Stumbling, off balance, Des's face lights up as he launches into you, his fist strikes your chin. Dazed, staggering backwards, shaking your head, you square up again and throw another punch, missing. Sucking in air, ignoring the throbbing in your jaw you ready yourself to try once more, until a roaring, like a steam-train furnace stops you in your tracks. Yanked backwards by the collar, your spun around to face Steve. 'What the bleedin' hell do you think you two are doing? Betty will give you both a hiding if she finds out. Ey?'

Des mutters, 'He started it.'

You ball your fists, the heat in your chest raging. 'C'mon, I'm not scared of you.'

Des snorts, 'I'll beat the shit out of you anywhere.'

Steve yells, 'Stop.' Gripping you both by the wrists, drawing you close, menthol and a hint of beer on his breath. 'If you two wanna fight, I'll arrange it, but not here, not in front of the house. Bugger me.' Shaking his head, he lets go and turns to walk back into the house. Pausing, over his shoulder, 'No more fighting, and get bloody well cleaned up.'

'There's blood on your chin,' Terry whispers as you push past.

Steve didn't take long to arrange a visit to the Police Boys Club in the heart of Marrickville. The officer who runs it, a friend of his, agrees that you can settle your differences in his boxing ring. Betty tut-tuts and shakes her head in disagreement when she finds out, but Steve silences her with a sharp look.

As you stand in front of the modest, brick building bathed orange from the dying sunlight, mixed emotions swirl. The desire to beat Des tugs at you, as does the idea that your skills might fall short. But the fury remains. *I won't run from him.*

The rhythmic thump of a ball resonates through the open door, along with laughter and shouts of glee. You enter behind Des, noting the worn floor, shivering at the sight of the boxing ring nestled in the corner. The canvas floor, once taut, sagging to the ground. Your chest constricts.

A uniformed officer approaches, shakes Steve's hand, introducing himself as Sergeant Doyle. His florid face cracks into a broad smile. 'These the lads?' At least one person is enjoying themselves. The sergeant's Irish brogue is music to your ears, a reminder of your mother's native tongue, but it prompts another shiver, for an entirely different reason.

Grinning, Steve says, 'Yeah. They reckon they can fight.'

'Grand. We'll see about that.' He laughs, a deep throaty sound from within his ample belly. The basketball players stop and stare, an expectant look on their faces; they know what's happening.

'Let's get the gear,' Sergeant Doyle says, escorting you both to a locker room, an old-school version, of sweat and liniment reminding you of gym sessions long ago. You sneak a look at Des, his face is drawn. *Is he worried?* Pumping an imaginary fist. *Maybe he's not as confident as he acts*. A pair of boxing gloves, their surface cracked and split, are handed to you. 'Steve, lace him,' the sergeant says, indicating Des. 'You boxed before?' he asks, taking your hands and slipping the gloves on. Shaking your head. 'Righto. These are the rules.' With a yank, he pulls the laces tight. Then, flexing the fingers on his right hand, as if to make a point, he cracks a knuckle one by one, rifle shots in the small room. 'Listen to my instructions and stop when I say so.' With a cautionary wave, adding, 'No hitting in the bollocks. Righto. Let's crack on.'

Fuck it. I'm going to hit him wherever I can.

The basketball players congregate on the benches. This is more thrilling than their usual Tuesday night, and they whisper and laugh as you climb into the ring—you're sure they're making bets, and not in your favour. Des marches to one corner, you to the opposite. His confidence appears to have returned. *Maybe he likes an audience.* You begin to understand why the canvas floor has buckled. The sergeant takes his place in the centre. 'Righto fellas, you can't fight from the corners. In the middle, and be sharpish about it.' Hands by your side, chewing your bottom lip, you walk to the centre of the ring and wait, staring at Des. His eyes are hard; he doesn't look away. You want to, but he'll see it as weakness. Your heart races. 'Hands up,' the sergeant shouts. 'Okay, box.'

You move around the ring, reminded of the punch on the chin as you look at Des, knowing it will be all over if he lands another like that. Des, with a snide look in his eye's steps toward you, throwing punch after punch at your stomach and ribs. You're protecting your head, each punch finds its target, knocking the wind out of you. Doubled over, dropping to one knee, sucking in oxygen. There's laughter from the benches. You grimace.

The sergeant pushes Des back and grips your shoulder with thick, calloused fingers. 'Jesus laddie, protect yourself,' he mutters, peering at you. 'Can you continue?'

You nod, gasping out, 'Yes.' Gritting your teeth, you get to your feet. All you need is to hit him once. Des waits with an air of nonchalance, knowing he has your measure. Treading warily, you move toward him and lash out, hoping the punch connects. He dodges it and returns with a punch flush to your chest. Staggering, your legs bend as if rubber, arms are lead weights. Des moves closer, his eyes signalling it's time to finish it. He throws punch after punch at your head, but in his haste, they whistle past your ears. With relief, you hear, 'Stop. To your corners lads.'

Staggering to the corner, Steve leans on the ropes and studies you. 'You alright? Want to keep going?' Nodding, too tired to speak. 'Right. Then for chrissake hold your hands up and move around the ring. Ey? You're making yourself an easy target.'

Grimacing, you want to say you're not doing it on purpose, but your mouth is busy sucking in air and it's all too much effort. A hollow feeling in your stomach grows as the sergeant calls you back to the centre.

'One more round lads, then shake hands. Okay?' You exhale. *I only have to survive one more round.* 'Okay, box.'

Des avoids your first punch. With a steely-eyed look he stalks you around the ring. *Don't wait, go after him.* You hurl a wild roundhouse punch, it catches him by surprise, connecting with his mouth, his lip splits open. Reeling back, a trickle of blood from his mouth. Your heart sings at the sight; energy flows through your veins. Des licks his lips, his tongue red, and throws a lacklustre punch. The sergeant calls a halt. Hands on knees, you gasp for air.

In the locker room, sinking to the bench you have a sense of satisfaction. The sergeant removes your gloves, squinting at you. 'I don't think boxing's your game lad. Best go home and stay out of trouble.' As you leave, glancing at the ring, a wry smile crosses your face. It doesn't look so frightening now. Des remains silent on the trip home, his only movement the occasional licking of his lips. You're swollen with pride, pleased with yourself and that you didn't back down.

≠

The bricks fly from your grip like a shotgun blast, scattering across the trailer bed with a clang. One finds its way onto the top of your foot, prompting a howl of pain. Laughter erupts from behind—Kevin leaning against the trailer, convulsing, while George is doubled over, clutching his belly.

You wince and turn away, your gaze shifting to the scattered bricks. Once again, you question why you'd agreed to this. It had been George's idea, or at least you think it was. At that moment, he'd been busy devouring a ham sandwich, his words muffled until he finally swallowed. Wrapping an arm around you and Kevin, he muttered something about a job.

'George, seriously, you stink.' Struggling to free yourself. 'What did you say about a job?'

He coughs, the sound disturbing to your ears, a shower of brick dust follows as he shrugs off his shirt. 'I recommended you and Kevin to my boss at the brickworks, for a job. He says come see him.'

'George, in case you didn't notice, we have jobs.' Kevin is silent—his face puckered up as if in pain. *What's bothering him?* George mumbles something else.

'What, what did you say?'

'I said, you both complain about your jobs.'

With a sigh, you concede, it's true. 'Kevin, what do you think? You wanna give it a go?' Absently, he nods, that strange look in his eyes. 'Looks like we're gonna work with you George.'

Beaming, slapping you on the back, he chortles, 'I knew youse would.'

You left the furniture factory due to a series of mishaps that raised concerns for Gary, also you were eager to escape Sharon, who made you feel like an outcast. You managed to pay Reg back, even though he seemed to value the gesture of buying him a beer more than the money.

Since then, you worked scraping solder off transistor radio circuit boards. The work is repetitive, matched only by the dreariness of the manager. He would stroll up and down the rows of desks, laid out like a classroom, occasionally halting to observe your work. Then, without invitation, he'd place his hand on your shoulder and let it linger until you squirmed in discomfort. Most recently you are mixing kitty litter in a large hopper.

'We'll have to quit George.'

'Best wait. The boss might not go for you.' Then, as he waltzed out of the room, he added, 'We need to arrive early tomorrow,' a cheeky smile on his face.

Trudging along Canterbury Road at five-thirty in the morning is the first time you regret saying yes. The second, as a passing garbage truck blew exhaust fumes all over you. Arriving at Canterbury Brickworks, you wait for the boss, Kevin begins moaning about George jumping on top of him and forcing him out of bed that morning. 'Do we have to leave so early every fuckin' morning?'

With a chuckle, George pounds him on the back. 'No. Today's special.'

Kevin, downcast, mumbles, 'So what do we do at this bloody job?'

George, flexing his arms, 'Load bricks on trucks. I can pick up six in one go, and that's not easy.' That was the end of the conversation, as a sleek limousine rolled up to the gate, and a man in a neatly fitting grey suit and matching tie got out. George leant across and whispered, 'Make sure you tell him how much you want the job.' But you were no longer sure you did, worried about how you were gonna lift six bricks.

Kevin voiced your sentiment. 'Not sure we fuckin' do.' You smile.

The man signalled to George. 'Are these them?' George nods, and you thought he was about to bow. 'Okay, let's get you signed up. George, get the gear they'll need.' George trots off across the yard, past a brick building, smoke pouring from its chimney, and enters a three-sided tin shed. You both follow the boss, who waves a sheet of paper. 'Fill this out. Payday is Friday. Days off are out of your wages. Boys, I need the trucks loaded and out every half-hour.' George returns, holding several pieces of rubber in his hands, the boss glances at him. 'George, show them what to do, and no slacking or mucking about.'

'Yes boss,' George says, again the thought he's about to bow before quickly ushering us away. 'C'mon, let's get started.'

You turn the rubber bits over in your hand, then tug on George's arm. 'What are these for?'

'Slip them over your fingers. The large piece fits into your palm. It protects your hands when you pick up the bricks, especially if they're straight out of the kiln. That's when they're bloody hot.' The more you hear about this job, the less you like it. Kevin tries to fit the rubber over his fist. 'Not like that, idiot,' George shouts in frustration. He slips the large rubber piece over his fingers, fitting it snugly in Kevin's palm. 'That's how you do it. Fuck me.'

You stare at the empty trailer, then at the stack of bricks. There were a lot of them. George began explaining what to do, but you aren't listening, the sheer number of bricks is on your mind.

'Hey, did you hear me?' George taps you on the top of your head.

Shrugging him away, you stared at the pile of bricks again, then at George. 'Do we have to load this many bricks every half-hour?'

He ignores you and continues: 'The trucks drop the empty trailer, and we go to each stack of bricks and put 'em on the trailer.' He paused, sweeping a lock of hair back from his face. 'There's an easy way to do it. Squeeze them together between your hands as you pick them up, then swing around and place them on the trailer. Okay, give it a go Graham.'

Now, foot throbbing, you have a third reason for not wanting this job.

You turn to Kevin. 'Bet you can't fuckin' do it.' He can't hide his delight at your pain.

George wipes his lips with the back of his hand. 'Let me show you.' In one swift motion, he picks up six bricks, swings around and places them on the trailer. 'Push them together as you lift. Don't do too many. Four is good to start with.'

Rubbing your foot, you say to Kevin, who's still smirking, 'So do it, smart-arse.' He gets four on the trailer without a problem. Muttering about the stupidity of this, you try again.

Kevin chuckles. 'Look, you made the trailer this time.'

'Fuck off.'

By the end of the day, Kevin and you are exhausted. You stumble home, head hanging, too tired to look up, arms weighing a ton, again wondering if you've made a mistake. The following day, neither Kevin nor you can move a muscle. Everything hurts. With a voice that lacks any sympathy, George says, 'You'll be okay once you get going.'

Kevin shakes his head. 'I'm not sure about that.'

Two weeks later, you're both loading bricks as if you've been doing it forever. Kevin and you develop arm muscles, which pleases him immensely. 'This'll make girls love me,' he says, flexing as we make our way home.

George, grinning, 'I reckon you'll need more than big arms to get a girl.' Kevin glares and lowers them. George continues, 'I heard Terry talking about a couple of girls he met. Maybe you could learn from him. He did say one of them is interested in you, Graham.'

You do a sudden about-turn and face him. 'What? Who? What?'

'Terry reckons you met 'em at Barn World. Says one is keen on you.'

'I don't ... I ...'

Kevin smiles, smacking you on the arm. 'You got a girl and you don't know it.'

'Uh, we talked to two girls at the checkout.' If you remember correctly, neither showed any interest in your presence. Still, a flutter of anticipation causes your heart to quicken. With a surge of urgency, you plead with Kevin and George to hurry home.

As you loiter outside the house, each passing second feels like an eternity, and you're aware of your impatience, tapping your foot as your eyes dart up and down the street searching for any sign of Terry. *Could George be right? Where the fuck is he?*

A figure catches your attention—strolling leisurely towards you. Running towards him, arms waving frantically, 'Terry! Hey, Terry.' The words tumble out. 'What's this? About two girls at Barn World?' His expression is one of surprise. A glint in his eye, 'Nice to see you too. Girls, what girls?'

In frustration, you grab hold of his shoulder. 'George said that you said ...'

Shaking you off, he breaks into a grin. 'Oh, them, yeah.'

'What the fuck do you mean, oh them?'

'I've seen one a couple of times. Dolly. She invited us to go to the beach tomorrow. Her friend asked if you wanted to go as well. But if you're coming you better act better than this, or forget it.'

You remember a girl with dark hair, but not much else. 'Are you sure?' Terry, shaking his head, walks away. Running after him, grabbing his elbow. 'How are we gonna get there?'

He smiles. 'Dolly has a panel van. She'll pick us up. Now fuck off and leave me alone.'

It's going to be a long wait until tomorrow.

You both wait in front of the house with an air of naughty schoolboys. For the past thirty minutes you've been grooming your hair, hoping it wouldn't defy gravity as it often did, and choosing what to wear.

Frustration got the best of Terry. 'A pair of shorts is all you need. Good grief, we're headed to the beach.' You want to tell him how important this is, but he turns away and leaves in a huff.

Terry, beach towel snugly draped around his waist and an aura of nonchalance is propped against the garden wall. You wonder if he's that unconcerned, noting the glisten of sweat on his forehead. Beads of sweat also run down your back, dampening your shirt. Discreetly sniffing beneath your armpit. *Do I smell?*

Terry, a query on his face, 'You right there?'

Ignoring the question, you try to remember the image of the girl. Despite your best efforts, nothing beyond the shade of her hair emerges. All other attempts prove fruitless.

Your anticipation grows as you see a van navigate the corner, creaking and groaning like a ship battling a stormy sea labouring up the hill. It comes to a shuddering halt on the opposite side of the street. The exhaust pipe rattles as the engine abruptly ceases with a loud bang. Terry moves closer. 'Make sure you get along with her.'

'How can I do that? That's stupid.' But he shushes you as the girls get out of the van, whispering and giggling. Your face reddens.

Terry constantly commented on Dolly's best feature, her breasts. They sway as she bounces across the street, then, with an exuberant shout, she covers the remaining distance and leaps into his arms. The second girl is slender, with suntanned legs. Freckles pepper her nose and cheeks. In a yellow sundress, she glows in your eyes. Adjusting your shirt, hoping your hair is in place, you smile.

Terry and Dolly's lips are still locked together, finally they part with a moist smacking sound. She rests her head on his shoulder, wears a contented smile. 'Hello Graham, nice to meet you.' Then, with a smirk, 'Graham this is Mary. Mary, say hello to Graham. All I've heard this week is "Graham this" and "Graham that".'

Mary squeals. 'Dolly, stop it.' She glances at you with a bashful smile. Mouth dry, you hang your head.

Dolly laughs. 'Stop acting like two school kids. C'mon, you'll both have to ride in the back.' Winking, 'And behave.' Mary squeals again.

Terry opens the rear door. 'Welcome to the shaggin' wagon.' There's a mattress on the floor, and a poster of Mario Milano plastered to the roof. Mary throws him a piercing look before climbing in. She takes in your glance at the poster. 'Dolly loves wrestling. Mario's her favourite.'

Terry glides across the front seat, stopping alongside Dolly, gently kissing her cheek. Dolly's neck flushes red. Mary giggles, quickly covering her mouth. Iron Butterfly booms from the eight-track as Dolly starts the motor. The music triggers memories of the hours you spent with

Craig. Lowering the volume, Dolly tosses a glance over her shoulder. 'Sorry about that. We're headed to Wollongong, so get comfortable.'

Mary intertwines her fingers with yours, the rumbling engine and clattering exhaust muffle make any attempt at conversation pointless. That doesn't bother you as you steal fleeting glances at Mary, reminding yourself this is really happening.

After an hour, Dolly slows the van, veering off the main road onto a sandy track. A glimpse of golden dunes and turquoise sea through the windshield. The van jostles and bumps along, there's a faint scraping sound along the sides of the van. Dolly brings it to a halt in an empty parking area.

With a grin, looking across at Terry, 'It's always deserted here. C'mon, the last one is chicken.' Tittering, she hops out, removes her blouse and shorts, a red and white striped bikini underneath. Then, with a wriggle of her breasts, she races away, puffs of sand are thrown up by her feet, squealing, she dives in and is swamped by a large wave. Terry rips off his jeans and T-shirt, grabs a towel and goes in hot pursuit.

Mary, more demure, removes her dress, revealing a black bikini and a cute pot belly. A coy smile crosses her face at your stare. You don't have swimmers; your pair of old work shorts will have to do. Dropping your T-shirt, you walk hand in hand to the water, enjoying the sensation of the warm sand between your toes.

Dolly splashes about like a baby seal. 'C'mon, hurry up.' Terry grabs her around the waist and dunks her under a wave. She erupts, spluttering, water streams off her now naked breasts. Arms across her chest, she screams, 'My top. Oh my god!'

He laughs. 'C'mon, show us, don't be shy.'

With a sly smile, she drops her hands. 'There, seen enough? Now find my fuckin' top.'

Scrabbling around on hands and knees in the surf, digging through the sand as you're buffeted by the waves, snatching at everything, only to catch bits of slimy seaweed. Terry stands and shouts, 'Got it,' waving the bikini top above his head. 'But if you want it, you gotta come and get it.' He races out of the water and up into the sand dunes, looking back over his shoulder, laughing. Dolly, close to tears, sits. Mary stares after Terry, lips pursed, a flash of annoyance in her eyes.

Sighing, knowing this might ruin your chances with Mary, you mutter, 'I'll go get it.' She glances at you with a grateful smile. There's a surge in your chest. *Does this mean she likes me?*

Catching up to Terry, 'You're being a prick. Give it back.'

'Rack off. I'll give it back when I'm ready.'

You rip it out of his hands. 'I'll take it back.'

'Can't anyone take a fuckin' joke?'

'It's not a joke to her.'

'I've fucked her you know.'

'Bullshit.'

'Why do you think there's a mattress in the van?'

'Does Mary know?'

Petulantly, he kicks at the sand. 'How would I know? I wanna do it again. So, if she wants to stop on the way back, youse betta disappear.'

You consider what he said. *If Dolly did, then maybe ...* 'How the fuck are we gonna disappear?'

He says nothing more as we return to the girls. You hand Dolly her top, and with a sheepish grin, Terry kisses her. The rest of the afternoon is spent lazing in the sun, spoiled only by Terry insisting Mary remove her top, complaining that everyone has seen Dolly's tits and we should see hers.

Annoyed, Dolly snaps, 'Stop it. Unless you prefer her to me?'

'No, never.' He wraps an arm around her waist, nibbles her neck.

She whimpers. Then, disentangling herself, stands, brushing sand from her legs, and winks at Terry. 'Let's go for a drive.'

You and Mary are back in the rear, providing another opportunity to hold hands. After the day's events, you feel game enough to put an arm around her shoulders, and she snuggles into your chest.

You pull up at a small bluff. Dolly, with a sideways glance at Terry. 'Would you like to go for a walk?' Before he can answer, she eyes us in the rear-view mirror. 'You two will be okay, won't you?' We both nod, happy to see them leave.

'They've done it, you know,' Mary says, as she watches them walk away, arms around each other's waist.

Pretending you don't understand, 'Done it. What do you mean?'

'You know. *IT*.' She places a hand on your leg. 'Do you like me?'

Trembling at the touch of her hand, you want to shout yes, but your mouth refuses to work properly, so instead you stutter, 'I, I'm ah, I ...'

'You don't sound like you do.'

'I'm, I do.' Hanging your head, whispering, 'I'm not good with girls.' This is not going the way you pictured. To convince her, you repeat, 'I, I do like you.'

A cautious expression on her face as she reaches behind, undoing the clasp of her bikini top, allowing it to drop into her lap. Your breath catches as disbelief washes over you. Your gaze fixed on her breasts, covered with the same freckles as her cheeks. They jiggle as she leans nearer, her tongue delves into your mouth. Tentatively, your hand brushes against her breast, enjoying its softness. Your fingers search for her nipple, encircling it. A soft gasp, then her fingers entwine in your hair, pulling your head down to her breast. You taste salt. Her other hand traces the swelling in your shorts, her grasp tightening as a wave of pleasure courses through you. Sliding your hand between her legs, her moans fill the air. Then, abruptly, she draws back, whispering, 'I can't.' Shoving you aside, she grabs her top, clasps it to her chest, flings open the van door, and runs in the direction of Dolly and Terry.

Stunned, a hollow feeling in your stomach. *What did I do wrong?*

Dolly, eyes blazing, comes running back to the van. 'What happened? Mary is crying her eyes out. What did you do?'

You raise your hands, shaking your head. 'I, we, we, uh, she got upset.'

Dolly calms, her face softening. 'Her old boyfriend came back last night. I think she's scared. Because she likes you.'

'Scared? Why? Should I talk to her?'

Dolly shakes her head. 'No. Not now. I will, later.'

Terry returns, Mary trails behind, sniffing, wiping a hand across her nose, her cheeks tear-stained. 'Sorry. I, I ...' she doesn't finish.

'Time to go,' he says, climbing into the rear with you. Mary sits in the front with Dolly. Her back remains taut throughout the drive home.

Standing on the pavement, watching the van roar away, you shake your head. It's the last time you expect to see her. *Fucking girls.*

≠

Weeks go by without a single message from Mary. You've made two trips to Barn World, hoping to catch a glimpse of her or Dolly, but both times they were nowhere to be seen. Terry's been with Dolly since the beach, but he brushes off your questions about Mary.

Sitting on the verandah, at a loss what to do next as the front door swings open, and Kevin emerges clutching a piece of toast.

'Betty's closing up, if you want any more brekky,' stuffing the toast into his mouth. Terry is close behind. 'Hey, you wanna go to Roselands?'

Your instinct tells you it's not a good idea, but you have no idea why. As always, Terry says there'll be girls. Pushing the doubts away, you glumly agree, unsure of why you're feeling unsettled.

Kevin pipes up, 'Great. I'll come.'

Terry nudges you, a warning glare on his face as he rolls his eyes. 'If you're coming, you're not wearing that stupid fuckin' hat.'

Kevin opens his mouth to argue, then gauges the look on Terry's face and shuts it again. 'Okay.'

'Thank fuckin' Christ.' You grin.

≠

As the entrance to Roselands glides open, chilly air greets you. This place is unlike any you've encountered before. Saturday morning must be a prime time for families. Children jump on and off plastic replicas of kangaroos and emus, ice cream smeared across their faces. A carousel spins to the tune of carnival music. A red and white striped awning swirls as the melody plays, with delighted squeals from those on board.

As your eyes gaze upwards, tracing level after level of shops, you notice chandeliers suspended from the ceiling, glistening as they capture the light. However, the most astonishing sight for you are the automatic stairs teeming with people going up and down.

≠

In Windhoek, a school mate's father owned a department store, but it paled in comparison. Musty clothes and unfamiliar items cluttered its counters, except for the fireworks display, a section you loved—memories of cracker night flooded back. Daniel didn't have many friends. He confided once that he believed it was because of his Jewish background. You didn't understand, simply nodding in reply. Your parents didn't object when you hung out with Daniel, although you recall your father's dismissive gesture upon learning you were spending cracker night at Daniel's.

You both collected as many fireworks as your arms could carry, grinning under the weight of Whizz Wheels, Shining Stars, Flower Pots, and Raging Infernos. The ultimate favourite was the Swallow Rocket. You recall planting it in a milk bottle, then scurrying away, half-expecting it to tip over and give chase. In Daniel's home, you felt safe.

Terry's grip on your arm startles you, pulling you out of your memories. His gaze directs your attention to a fountain. Cascading water down its edges pours into a pond enclosed by a low brick wall. Yet, it's not the design that captures his interest—or yours. It's the trio of girls near the fountain. All three have short-cropped hair, and are wearing miniskirts and knitted jumpers. In hushed tones, he says, 'I've seen them before,' he shakes his head. 'Fuck 'em. Let's head upstairs.'

Making your way through the crowd, thrilled at having a chance to step onto the moving stairs. Your smile spreads from ear to ear as you ride to the top. Hopping off, you pause outside a men's store, captivated by the pants and floral shirts on display. For one moment you imagine yourself wearing them. With a shake of your head. *That's never going to happen.*

Your clothes are from a salesman who arrived on the doorstep, claiming fantastic clothing at budget prices. He guided you towards a parked white van across the street. That should have raised your suspicions, but you and the other boys couldn't help but feel excited about the prospect of new clothes. The salesman swung open the van's rear doors, revealing an assortment of shirts and pants neatly stacked in cardboard boxes—perhaps that should have been another clue. As you check out the clothing, he proposes a payment plan allowing you to pay weekly. Agreeing, you buy a pair of corduroy flared pants and a cheesecloth shirt with white and blue stripes.

From that point, the salesman would turn up every Friday afternoon like clockwork for his money. Unsure of how much it cost, you suspect you ended up paying more than the items were genuinely worth—particularly after discovering that Betty had been the one to recommend his visit.

With a shake of your head, you turn away, doubting you'll ever find yourself shopping in a place like that.

Kevin wheezes, his face coated with a plasticine sheen. Terry notices and suggests he sits. Kevin nods, slumping onto a bench, placing his head between his hands. You exchange a worried glance with Terry, and are about to suggest going home when he nudges you. 'It's them.'

'Who?'

'The girls from downstairs.' You take a greater interest now and study them.

Kevin raises his head. 'Girls? What girls?'

Terry, ignoring him, 'Let's see if they follow. You okay Kevin?' He nods, still looking around for the girls.

They're standing near the stairs, heads close together. Passing close by we get a good look at them; one glances up and smiles at Kevin. He moves toward her and says something. Her back stiffens, she whispers to the other two and they stalk off. Terry, face reddening, growls, 'What the fuck did you say to them? You've pissed them off.'

'Fuck off. I only said hello.'

Furious, he barks, 'Let's go to the fountain. If they turn up, keep your fuckin' mouth shut Kevin.'

They're not at the fountain, not that you expected them to be—you figure they've gone home. Terry shrugs. 'Let's wait. Maybe they'll turn up. If they do, someone needs to keep quiet.' Clenching his jaw, glaring at Kevin.

Kevin ignores him, his wheezing worse. 'How long we gonna stay?'

Terry shoots him a withering stare, muttering under his breath. Then you hear a sharp intake of breath from him. Hoping it's the girls arriving, you spin your head around, but unable to see them, turn back to Terry. 'What is it? What's up?'

His face has a green hue, mouth open as he indicates something above. Looking up, your blood runs cold. Lining the railing, eyes fixed on the three of you, are Sharpies, a lot of them. And the three girls are with them.

'Fuckin' hell,' he says in a low voice. 'This is trouble, I ...' He stops abruptly as five descend the stairs in unison, arranging themselves in a semicircle before you. A thin boy with a pitted and pockmarked face, skin so pale it appeared to be luminous, veins prominent on his arms, took a step forward. His expression mirrored one reserved for stumbling upon something disgusting on the sole of a shoe. The remaining four stare at you with eyes as unyielding as flint. Fear rises, causing a shudder as memories of a past encounter in Africa come rushing back.

≠

Your brother and his friend had set out to find blackberries, deliberately leaving you behind. Undeterred, you tag along, staying far enough out of reach to not cop another smack across the head, eventually losing sight of them. Climbing a small kopje, you hope to locate them. But the sun's heat saps your energy, and with no trace of your brother or his friend, you lie in the shade of the one and only tree sticking out of a rock crevice. The kopje provides a warm sensation against your back and you gradually fall asleep.

A loud grunt jolted you awake. Raising your head, you freeze as a group of baboons, led by a large male, appear from the opposite side of the hill. The male emits a roar, vibrating from his chest, before dropping to all fours and clambering towards you.

You bolt, cascading and tumbling down the kopje until you find yourself headfirst on the ground. In a daze, scrambling to your feet you continue sprinting, disregarding the thorn bushes tearing at your legs. Over your shoulder, you see that the baboon has halted, standing erect on its hind legs. It growls, mouth wide open, yellow fangs gleam menacingly.

≠

Shaking your head to free yourself of the memory, sweat courses down your spine. The air is tense, matched by Terry's silence. Kevin anxiously gnaws on his lower lip. The semicircle around you tightens as the pale boy edges closer. 'Youse cunts tried to pick up our girls?' A flicker of disgust in his eyes as he focuses on Terry. 'Wadda you doin' with these long hair shits?'

Terry shakes his head. 'We weren't doing nuthin'.'

You sneak a look at Kevin, then whisper in his ear. The boy leans forward, his nose inches from yours. 'What are you fuckin' whispering about, prick?'

You nod towards Kevin. 'He's finding it hard to breathe. Let him go, we'll stay.' Terry slides towards you to say something, but with a shake of your head you stop him.

Cunning eyes look at you, then at Kevin, then back at you. 'Alright. He can fuck off. But you two aren't going anywhere.' Watching Kevin go, your heart sinks. The look in the boy's face is one of triumph, he knows you're now at his mercy.

Terry repeats, 'We didn't do anything.'

'You wanted to fuck us,' one of the girls yells out, the Sharpies burst into snide laughter.

Another girl shouts, 'Your fucking dogs.'

'Is that right? Did you wanna fuck 'em?'

Shaking your head, 'No.'

He's close enough to you to be able to count the pockmarks, and smell the beer on his breath. Sensing something is about to happen, the four flex their arms. 'Come outside,' he snarls. 'Or you chicken?'

You've no intention of leaving, and you don't believe Terry wants too either. It's nearly midday, and the centre is beginning to empty, nobody takes any notice of you or the boys surrounding you. *I hope Kevin hurries.* 'Against all of you? I don't ...'

He cuts you off. 'Chicken shits. Tell you what. If you can beat one of us, we'll let you go.' His laugh is chilling. You remember the park in Campsie. They'd never let you do that. He becomes agitated, sweat rolls down his cheeks, he lowers his voice. 'You think you're better than us. Don't you?'

Suddenly there's a yell from above, startling everyone. Tensing, *What now?* The pale boy looks up in disbelief as another makes his way hurriedly down the stairs. 'Fuck me, is that Terry?' A weak smile crosses Terry's face as the Sharpie grabs his hand, pumping it up and down. 'I haven't seen you in ages. What've you been up to?'

Terry grins. 'Craig. How are you?'

Craig turns to look at the Sharpies as they pour down the stairs like a swarm of locusts. All with a mixture of surprise and curiosity on their faces due to the unexpected turn of events. You find yourself in disbelief, struggling to grasp what's happening. *Is this another trick?*

'I crossed paths with Terry during my time with the Town Hall crew,' Craig's expression turned into a smile. 'We rolled this old piss head. Terry ended up getting caught but never dobbed on us.' The tension miraculously disappears as they greet Terry as an old friend, shaking his hand and patting him on the back. However, the pale-faced boy has none of it. His lips part in a snarl, his anger simmering, realising that the opportunity to beat the shit out of you slipping through his fingers.

The girls feel the same. 'What about us?'

Craig yells, 'Shut the fuck up.' Taking Terry's arm, 'You wanna come with us?' He winks, nodding at the girls.

Terry shakes his head. 'No. I better get going.'

'If you change your mind, you're welcome. It'll be like old times.' You hear him say, in a quieter voice, 'Don't bring the others.'

As you move away, the pale boy sneaks up alongside. A glance at him brings back the image of the large baboon. You half-expect him to start drooling. 'You got lucky. There were more of us outside, ready to bash your fuckin heads in,' he remarks. You picture him watching, laughing, and delivering a kick while you're down on the ground. As the doors of Roselands shut, you shiver.

George, Kevin and Neal are running across the car park. Neal shouts, 'You okay?' His face flushed, body tense, ready for a fight.

'Yeah. Terry knew one of them. But thanks for coming.'

Terry, turns to you, 'Was that what you said to Kevin?' You nod.

Neal claps you on the back. 'Gotta take care of each other.' Words you've heard before.

≠

It was when the police turned up at the house—not a completely unusual event. Kevin, Terry and you stay out of the way until they leave. Betty is in the kitchen, leaning against the sink, eyes red from crying.

Kevin is the first to speak. 'What's wrong?'

'Peter's in hospital. They don't think he'll live.'

Shocked, we all spoke at once. 'What?' 'How?'

She sobs. 'He was beaten up on his way home.' Tears, fat and heavy, roll down her cheeks, plopping onto the linoleum. Neal, hearing the commotion, joins us. Betty, wipes a hand across her face, sighs. 'I'm going to bed. You boys get your own lunch.'

As she left, Neal, in a gruff voice, says, 'We gotta take care of each other.' We share a solemn silence.

Terry spoke up. His voice, a mixture of frustration and resentment. 'I'm willing to bet it's those Campsie

Sharpies. They're nothing but a bunch of pricks.' The memories of the incident in the park resurfaces, the emotions still raw. Terry continued, 'I can get a car.'

Neal nods. "Okay, let's do this. But we mustn't let Betty know."

Terry reappears in the evening with a four-door Corolla. Neal emerges, holding a baseball bat, his face a picture of grim resolve. 'Time to go,' he declares, slipping into the front, the bat finding its place under the seat.

All we find is a young boy on a pushbike. Neal and the baseball bat petrify him so much that he wets his pants. Neal let him go.

Peter died the next day. His passing casting a shadow over everything, compounded by his family's request—for us not to attend the funeral.

≠

Reflecting on these memories, it's astonishing that you emerged without a scrape. How you managed to avoid the Sharpies leaves you utterly amazed. While you want to credit your survival to careful planning, deep down, you acknowledge that the reality is far more intricate. There's a sense that you were protected, how, or by what, you cannot explain.

What's clear is that following the showdown with the Sharpies at Roselands, a newfound self-assurance took root. This belief in yourself is vital as you sense greater challenges on the horizon.

≠

Trouble is inevitable with seven adolescent boys confined in the same house. The situation worsens when Alfie and Kevin get into a heated argument over a Weet-Bix. It escalates to the point where Betty has to step in, tearing the Weet-Bix into halves and hurling them into their respective bowls. 'There, now eat it, for heaven's sake.' Alfie grumbles, retreats to his bedroom, slamming the door shut and leaving his half untouched. Kevin eats both.

As you leave the dining room, a thong zips past your ear before rebounding off the wall and hitting your head. Swiftly turning around, Terry stands behind you with a grin.

'Fuck. What the hell?'

'I hate spiders.' The spider in question scuttles away, unharmed.

'What's wrong with you? You've been shitty all week.'

Distracted, fiddling with his shorts. 'I'm leaving.'

You've heard it before. In fact, all of you've said it at one time or another. Well, apart from Alfie—although that might change after the Weet-Bix.

'Betty says if I go, she won't take me back.' He stops, stares off into the distance, a mournful look on his face. 'She reckons I'll do something stupid.'

'She's probably right. Where will you go?'

Terry grimaces. 'Yeah, s'pose. I'd like to go see me mum, see how she is. I also need to get away from Dolly. She wants to be with me all the time. Deadset accuses me of being with someone else when I'm not.' Pausing, slipping on his thong, 'Fuckin' sheilas.'

One week has passed since that conversation. Now, while you're having breakfast, he strolls in like he's never left. 'What, where've you ...?'

Interrupting, he smirks, 'With Dolly.' A silly grin on his face as he reaches for the Froot Loops, shaking the box, groaning, 'It's empty.' Looking around. 'Anymore?'

'Did you see your mum?'

With a shake of his head, 'Nah, she wasn't home. I didn't hang around in case the old prick caught me. Bastard would've called the police, like last time. I met up with Dolly.'

'You're back with her. You said she pisses you off.'

He leans across the table. 'Yeah, she does, but ...' He shakes the box again. 'Bloody hell, I'm hungry.'

Irritated, you snap, 'But what?'

He scoffs, changing the subject. 'I got news. Mary broke up with her boyfriend.'

Biting your lip, the tempo of your heart increases, 'Did she? Is she?'

'Dolly reckons they got into a big fight about her dad. Anyway, you're not interested. Are you?'

'Um, if she ...'

Terry hits his palm against his forehead with a loud smack. Chuckling, 'Course you're not. I can ask if you want.'

Do I want to? Memories flood you. The recollection of holding her in your arms, the taste of salt on your lips from her breast. Cheek's flushing, you lower your head concentrating on your cereal, attempting to control the flurry of sensations. Releasing a sigh, conceding, 'I suppose.'

Terry exclaims, 'For fuck's sake,' and stomps into the kitchen.

≠

Dolly is perched on the van's bonnet, observing you both as you draw near. Gracefully uncrossing her legs, she slides to the ground. Straightening her skirt, wrapping Terry in her arms. She shoots a playful wink your way over his shoulder. 'Hello, Graham. Searching for Mary. Hoping she might burst out from the rear?' She giggles, amused by the disappointment on your face. Perhaps feeling sorry for you, she adds, 'We'll pick her up from her place, don't worry.'

Mary is waiting in front of her house, skittish, like a newborn pony. Her eyes darted between her home and the street. As the van stops, you swing the door open and rush over, a familiar hollowness in your stomach. She steps back, placing her hand on your chest.

'Quick, let's go ...' Moving past you, she squeezes into the front seat next to Terry. Feeling disheartened, you climb into the rear. The Rolling Stones have replaced Mario Milano.

'I know a spot,' Dolly shouts over the rattling engine. 'Not many people go there.' The clamour from the engine prevents any more conversation. After a while, she steers onto a rugged dirt track and brings the van, with a bang and shudder, to a halt at a grassy clearing. A chain-link fence and a padlocked gate stop any further progress. You understand why it's deserted. A sign bears the words, 'Unauthorized Entry Prohibited. Sewage Plant.'

Dolly grins. 'It's quiet, if you don't mind the smell.'

Mary, twirling a strand of hair between her fingers, looks at you with a shy smile, 'We can stay in the van.' Turning away, her face reddening.

Dolly prods Terry. 'They want to talk.' She winks, they leave, disappearing behind a clump of trees.

Mary climbs into the rear, one eyebrow raised. 'You upset with me?'

'Um … no.' You're picturing her freckle-covered breasts.

'You know I broke up with my boyfriend.'

'Uh, oh, yes, Terry told me. Sorry.'

'Nah, don't be. I only went with him to spite my dad.'

Her fingers trace up your forearm. You try to focus on her words, but your thoughts are whirling. Leaning in, she kisses you. Fingers trembling, you reach over and begin undoing her buttons, frustrated by one refusing to undo. With a light titter, she undoes it. Your hand slips beneath her shirt and over her breast, cupping it. She moans, 'Take them off.'

You unzip, her warm breath against your cheek. She removes her panties, flicking them aside. Her tongue runs down the side of your neck, and then, with a mischievous glint in her eyes, she climbs on top, guiding you inside. You cry out in pleasure as a tingling sensation begins in your toes and races up your spine until it seems to surge from the top of your head. Her shrieks vibrate against the van's interior.

Pausing, worried you've hurt her, she shouts, 'Don't stop.'

Lying arm in arm, soaking up the moment, she breaks the silence. 'We should get dressed.'

'No. I like lying here like this.'

She giggles. 'I know what you like.'

There's a holler from Dolly. 'Hey, are you two ready to go home?' Followed by a thump on the side of the van.

Collapsing into fits of laughter, Mary, wipes a tear from her eye, shouts back, 'Yes.' Clutching her panties in one hand, straightening her skirt with the other, she glances at you. 'Do you wanna ...?' Before she can finish, the van door opens, Terry and Dolly stand there, grinning.

'You two finished talking?' There's an innocent smile on Dolly's face. 'If so, we should get going.'

You hold Mary all the way home, kissing her as she hops out. 'See you soon,' she says, waving goodbye.

As you and Terry walk down the driveway, stars emerge, twinkling and sparkling, mirroring your heart.

Opening the front door, it jams against an olive duffel bag. Puzzled, stepping over the bag, you hear Betty's voice, harsh and cold, echoing in the hallway. You've never heard her speak like this before. Exchanging a glance with Terry, a question in your eyes. Raising his shoulders, a shake of his head.

Around the table, George and Kevin sit on one side, heads bowed, while Alfie and Des occupy the opposite side. Neal sits at one end, pallid, red-rimmed eyes meeting yours fleetingly before he lowers his head, his forearms tremble.

Betty, with her elbows on the table. 'You're home. Sit down.' You both pull out chairs. 'Yes, there, anywhere.' Her face is as hard as stone. *What's going on?*

Betty, in a voice that carries clearly across the room, 'Neal's leaving. He ... he's ...'

Alfie pipes up. 'Leaving. Leaving. No. No. No leaving.'

Betty chops her hand down onto the table. 'Quiet Alfie. You're not leaving.' Alfie slinks down in his chair, confused, a hurt look in his eyes. Neal continues to stare at the table, his fingers pick at a hole in the plastic cover.

Terry looks at Betty, then at Neal. 'What's going on?'

Betty, spittle on her chin, snaps, 'You want to tell them, or shall I?'

You shrink in your seat, not understanding what's happening, but the hate in her voice triggers deep fears. It's your father all over again.

Neal remains silent. 'Well, if you're not gonna, I will.' Taking a deep breath, she spits out. 'Neal's a poofter. There was a boy in his room last night.' *I did see something.*

Her words descend in the room like a hammer strike. Betty's rage is unmistakable, evident in her eyes and the rise and fall of her chest beneath her worn housecoat. Her voice pierces the air, 'This will not be tolerated under my roof.' Her palm strikes the table. In terror, you refrain from looking up, instead, stare at a tomato sauce stain, deliberately avoiding any connection with Betty or Neal. Abruptly pushing her chair back, she strides out. You hear Neal say something in a hushed murmur and his chair scraping. The urge to ask him to stay is strong, but you remain silent. The front door clicks shut.

A wash of shame envelops you as you realise your cowardice, the self-assurance you had fades into nothingness, consumed by fear. Your heart aches, both for Neal and for yourself. But it's not the first time you've ignored a friend in need.

≠

You and Paul, a friend from school, find yourselves in Ken's 68 Falcon station wagon driving along Bagot Road. You're not close to Ken, this is your only memory of being with him in Darwin. He's unsettled, frequently checking the rear-view mirror. Turning around, you spot the Roberts brothers in a car trailing behind. They signal for Ken to pull over.

Paul, visibly shaken, confides, 'It's me they're after. Something happened involving their sister, and they threatened they'd get me.'

You're filled with fear, yelling at Ken to head back to Paul's house. 'They won't do anything there.' Instead, he turns onto Macmillan Road and pulls into a narrow dirt lane adjacent to a cemetery. Anxious and frustrated. 'Why are you fuckin stopping? Keep going.'

Ken's expression is sombre. 'They're my cousins.' The Roberts brothers pull up behind, blocking any escape. A troubling thought crosses your mind. *Did he arrange this?*

One of the Roberts brothers yanks the car door open and leans in. 'I promised I'd get you, you bastard. Let's settle this.' Resignedly, Paul gets out. The brothers hurl a series of blows at him, despite his attempts to evade them, they batter his face into a raw, bloody mess. Dragging him back to the car and unceremoniously dumping him onto the rear seat. 'Take the cunt home.' With that, they drive away, their laughter echoing after them.

≠

Betty kicking Neal out of the house brought back painful memories. A shudder racks your body as you recall the anger and hate in her voice. Relieved now that you have someone you can talk to about it. Another glance toward Barn World—still no movement. *She has to finish soon.*

While you wait impatiently, your mind drifts to your heated disagreement with Terry earlier in the day. The irritation from that encounter still rankles.

He was searching for something in your wardrobe when you approached him. Poking his head out, 'Have you seen my sneakers?'

'Fuck off. They're not here.'

Grumbling, 'Shit. Where are they then?'

'You didn't mean that stuff about Neal, did you?'

'Yes. How could he stay after what he did? Jeez, where the fuck are they?' Going back to his search.

Annoyed by his attitude, 'You're a shithead. What about Roselands? He came to help.'

A muffled reply about not needing him came from the cupboard. Terry stamps out of the room without another word, and without his sandshoes—which you know full well, are on Kevin's feet.

Mary skips across the road. Watching her, your heart aches. You attempt to give her a kiss, but she pulls away. 'No, not here, my boss might see.'

Pursing your lips, sulking, 'Where then?'

Giggling, fluttering her eyelashes, 'Don't be mad. The park's quiet, and I've brought something for you.'

'Did you? What?'

'C'mon. I'll show you.'

Sneaking a sidelong glance, your chest pulses with delight. You find it difficult to believe it's you she likes.

You hurry through the park, past an elderly couple on a bench sitting quietly, hands intertwined, while a gentle wind tousles the woman's overcoat. The man draws her closer, nestling her against his chest. A family of ducks sound an alarm, their squawks filling the air as they rush back to the safety of the pond.

Mary, grasping your hand, leads you towards a large shrub near an empty playground. 'No-one will see us here.' She tugs on her skirt, wrapping it around her legs as she sits, taking a packet of Lemon Crisps out of her bag. 'Do you like these?'

'Uh, sure.'

'You expected something else?' Her face is a mirror of virtue.

Casting your eyes down, you take the offered biscuit, covering up your embarrassment. Then begin to tell her about Neal. Tears prick in the corners of your eyes as you relay the events. Brushing them away, 'I should've said something.'

The colour drains from her face. Averting her gaze, picking at a stalk of grass, 'I'm glad you didn't, or you ...'

'I let him down.'

'If you'd said something, you might have been thrown out too. Then we ...' Moving closer, sliding a hand between your legs. 'Then we couldn't do this.'

Thoughts of Neal, Betty and Terry vanish in the blink of an eye, a white-hot heat replacing them. Gasping, 'We can't, not here, I ...'

Smirking, she continues to squeeze and whispers in your ear, 'I missed you.' Pulling your zipper down, her hand slides inside. Your lips press against hers, a tingle in your spine. Breathlessly, she murmurs, 'You want to?' Throat tight, you nod.

The old couple are still there, but neither look in your direction, none the wiser of your presence. The ducks have reappeared, continuing to feed on the grass—you don't think they'll mind.

Mary kicks off her shoes, reaches under her skirt and pulls off her panties. You catch a glimpse of black hair. 'Get them off,' she says, tugging at your pants.

Wriggling, you wrench them down over your hips. 'Shit, they won't ...'

Laughing, she shoves them to your ankles. 'You look ready.' A guttural moan from deep inside as she takes hold. Placing a finger on your lips. 'Shhh.' Her breathing heavy. 'Quick, get on top.' Fumbling, unable to put yourself inside, she cries out, 'Move up,' arching her back.

'I can't ... it's not ...'

Taking hold, she slides you inside, your mouth drops open in pleasure. 'Oh, fuck, yes.' Her fingernails dig into your shoulders as you hang onto each other.

You remain on top not wanting the moment to end. With a snort she rolls you off. 'I have to go. My dad will worry if I'm late.'

'You free tomorrow?'

Giggling, she leers, 'You want more? C'mon, get up.' Flicking away the leaves stuck to her skirt and patting it down, she glides her tongue along her lips, stifling a chuckle at the look on your face. As you walk back in the twilight, the elderly couple have vanished, as have the ducks, you let out a long sigh. The world is right again.

'Where do you catch the bus?'

'Over there,' nodding at a bus shelter across the street, next to a dilapidated phone box. 'Oh hell, look, it's coming.'

Laughing as you run through the park hand in hand, arriving ahead of the bus. Brakes squeal as it comes to a grinding halt. Clambering up the steps, paying the driver, Mary takes a window seat and blows you a kiss. With a hiss of brakes, the bus moves away.

Sauntering home, you feel giddy and light-headed. The banging of pots and pans from the kitchen sounds more enthusiastic than usual for Betty. You hear her muttering to herself. Hoping nothing else has happened and brimming with curiosity, you join her in the kitchen.

'Where'd you go? I've been waiting,' she snaps.

Taken aback by her abrupt manner, 'I, um ...'

'You had a visitor.'

Confused, you don't understand. 'A visitor.' You repeat. 'Who?'

'Your father.'

Her words are a meat cleaver to your heart. The colour drains from your face; your legs go weak. Shaking your head, 'No. No. He can't. No. Not here.'

Betty stares, a flicker of sympathy on her face. 'Well, he was. Standing there, where you are, not more than an hour ago.' She turns away, rummaging in a cupboard. 'Ah, found you,' pulling out a black pot. 'He wants to talk to you. He gave me ... where is it?' Banging the pot onto the stove, searching in her apron pocket, 'Here,' holding up a crumpled business card.

Shaking your head, still unable to believe it. 'What? How?'

'He asked you to call. There's a number on the back, I think. Now shoo, dinner won't make itself.'

You sense her gaze piercing your retreating back. Shock grips you like a noose constricting your throat.

≠

Frustration courses through you. Your hands tighten into clenched fists as you stride back and forth on the same pavement where not even a day has passed since you last stood. Questions whirl in your mind. *Where in the world is she? He wants me to call*, shaking your head. *No, I won't. How did he find me? Why now?* Lost in your thoughts, you're oblivious to her presence.

'You okay? A worried look creases her brow.

'Let's go to the park and I'll tell you.'

Settling on the grass, taking hold of your chin, her eyes search yours. 'What's wrong? Tell me.'

'I'm ... my dad, he, umm, he turned up ... at, at the house.'

Her eyes glisten. 'How? I mean ...' Shaking her head. 'I didn't think he knew where you were.'

'He doesn't, didn't. I, I don't ...' Running your hands through your hair, realising how close you'd come to seeing him. You don't know what to say. Emotions are running wild in you. 'He spoke to Betty.'

Placing her arm around your waist, she squeezes, murmuring, 'It'll be alright.'

Your shoulders slump because you know that's not true. 'No, it won't.'

'What then? What will you do?' You don't have an answer, but her face mirrors your grief. Taking your hand, pressing it against her cheek, 'How did you end up here? In the house with the others?'

'Umm ...'

You know she's trying to distract you from your thoughts, but recalling past events makes you shudder. 'Tell me about your father?'

How can I? I don't know him. Resting your head on her shoulder, you start where you think it began. 'My father didn't care about me. I could never please him.'

'What do you mean, didn't care?'

Sighing, you don't want to go over this, you have a thousand times, but you owe her an explanation.

She runs her fingers along your cheek. 'Did he hit you?'

Pausing momentarily, 'It's hard to explain, he did, but ....' The weight of guilt rests on you. Focusing on the pond, its surface ruffles from a breeze, forming tiny ripples. The absence of ducks is notable.

Your voice is distant, as your mind wanders back to memories of that afternoon in the forest. Tentatively, you try to put the past into an order she might understand. 'I was five the first time, for taking two toy helicopters from a shop. He'd get provoked by everything I did.'

Hand over her mouth, a tear down her cheek. Her reaction makes you feel it's safe to tell her more. She slips her hand in yours. 'Is that why you left?'

'It wasn't ... I never ....' You glance at her, and there's a sad expression in her eyes. If you stop now, you'll never finish, so you continue. 'I didn't feel I belonged. I know it's an odd thing to say, but that's how I felt. I was happier on my own. I'd rather play in the woods than be at home. There, I always walked on eggshells in case he'd explode.'

Squeezing your hand, 'Why didn't they stop you from leaving?'

It's a question you've asked yourself more than once. Your cheeks flush, and you divert your eyes, shaking your head. Revisiting the pain causes you to cringe. *How to explain?* Seeking sympathy isn't your intention. Your lip quivers, 'I couldn't live at home any longer. I'd had enough, so I left, and they didn't stop me. He found me once when I stayed in a men's hostel. I had to leave there too.' *I'll tell her more another time.*

She gasps. 'That's awful.'

Shaking your head, 'No. Not, not really.'

Her fingers caress your arm. 'How'd you end up here?

With a shrug, 'A friend wanted to visit his sister, here, in Sydney. But we ended up arguing and he left.' Remembering the following days, and the close encounters you'd had. 'I've always believed that I was protected. That sounds strange, hey.'

'Protected? What do you mean? How?'

You consider what your about to say. There were all these things that ought to have hurt or even killed you, yet didn't. 'In Africa, as a kid, I was chased by baboons. If they'd managed to catch up to me...' Your voice fades as you recollect that particular day. 'A snake lunged towards me, but miraculously, a rock moved and trapped it an inch from my ankle. I also survived a serious car crash.' Grinning, you continue, 'When I needed help, Kevin appeared and I came out unscathed from two encounters with Sharpies. So, here I am.'

You glance across. There's a strange look in her eyes—not disbelief, more concern, as if she thinks you may be crazy. *Perhaps she's right.*

'I know it sounds strange, but this might convince you.' Cohen had been absent from your thoughts for a long time. The events deeply unsettled you, even though you were far away when they happened.

'In Africa I had this close friend, Cohen. As his birthday approached, he told me his father had something special in store for him. He wanted me to be there. Unfortunately, we returned to England a month before his birthday.

One night, my father entered the bedroom, and said, "They've sent me this from Africa," holding a piece of newspaper aloft. He read it out loud. Cohen's father had arranged for a plane to take him on a joy flight for his birthday. However, the plane crashed, killing Cohen and the pilot. Cohen's father witnessed it all.

My father used this to emphasise a point, mainly because I'd protested about leaving Africa before Cohen's birthday. He dropped the newspaper clipping onto the bed and left without uttering another word. If circumstances had been different and my family had remained, I might have also been on that plane.' Shrugging, 'Maybe I should have been.'

She shakes her head but remains silent, hunched over, twisting a blade of grass between her fingers. Then she whispered, 'Do you ... do you wanna go back?' You don't want to answer. She sniffs, wiping her nose with a tissue that appears from under a sleeve. 'Are you gonna call? Now he knows where you live, he'll come back. Won't he?'

'I guess. Would you come if he wants to see me?'

'Won't he want to see you on your own?'

'Fuck that. Please come.'

'Is he coming back to the house?'

'Shit no.' Taking the crumpled card out of your pocket, offering it to her. 'He left a number on this.'

She turns it over in her hand, as you had. 'There's a room number as well. See?'

Taking it from her fingers, 'Don't matter. I'm not gonna call.'

'There's a phone box over there. You can call now.'

Shaking your head, 'No.' *I'm not ready to talk to him. He'll make me go back.* 'I don't ... I can't, he'll ...'

'You can't ignore him. I'll be with you.' She stands, extending her hand. 'C'mon.'

'Can't. Got no money.'

'If you wait any longer, I'll have to go. I've gotta get home and feed me rabbit.

Mum and Dad got her for me. I wanted a lamb but they said no and got me a rabbit.'

The park has a desolate atmosphere at this moment. Your steps are heavy as you reach the phone box, with a sensation akin to a condemned man walking to the gallows. Mary, pulling at your arm, does nothing to lift your spirits. A hollow sense in your stomach as you spy the metallic and glass phone box, its orange sign displaying 'Payphone'. But it might as well declare 'Your Worst Nightmare.'

She nudges you, bringing you back to reality. 'You can't call him from outside,' she remarks. She doesn't waiver in the face of the withering look you give her. Instead, she hands you four twenty-cent coins. They rattle as they rest in your palm. You reach for the door. It opens with a shrill screech.

Before you can step inside, Dolly pulls up in her van, yelling across the street, 'Mary, glad I found you. Your dad wants you home. He's pissed off.'

Mary waves a hand, motioning to Dolly, now crossing the street, to be quiet. 'Graham's dad turned up. He's gotta call him.'

A flicker of hope in your chest. If Mary has to leave, you can avoid calling. A smile on your lips, swiftly wiped away in case she notices. In a low voice, 'I can call later. If you gotta go.'

Putting her hands on her hips, shaking her head, 'No. If you want me to meet him, call now. Dolly can wait. Anyway, she loves a bit of gossip.' Icy fingers trace a path along your spine, you know you're defeated.

The phone box has discarded cigarette ends on the floor, a coiled mass of hardened brown shit in one corner. A large crack in the handset, a frayed cable, barely connected it to the phone. A surge of joy, a chance it might not work. With a trembling hand, you lift the receiver. Mary pounds on the glass, silently urging you to hurry up. Placing the phone against your ear, the sound that greets you is a dial tone, and your final glimmer of hope dies. Sliding two twenty-cent coins into the slot, you dial the number on the back of the card.

A polite male voice on the other end says, 'The Menzies. Can I help you?'

'Uh, yes. I'm, uh, can you put me through to room four two one. Oh, sorry, that's four, two, se ... seven?'

'Room four two seven. One moment please.'

A heavy silence hangs in the air, a sudden crackle and a click. You struggle to contain the impulse to hang up. And then, your father's voice.

≠

The phone box door clatters closed. The business card, damp with sweat, sticks to your hand, while the remaining coins lie heavy in your pocket. Mary hurries over, wrapping you in her arms.

'What did he say? Tell me.'

Pushing her away. 'Shit, let me breathe.'

'Sorry.' With an expectant glance, Dolly moves closer, ensuring she doesn't miss a word.

'He wants me to go see him tonight.'

'Tonight!' Mary's hands flutter like a butterfly's wings.

'Yeah, he's here for one more night. Some conference or something.' Your laugh is brittle. 'He waits until it's convenient. Fuck him.'

Mary grabs your shoulders, a mad look in her eyes that you haven't seen before. 'Stop it. I didn't think you wanted to see him, and now you're angry with him?'

Dolly, unable to contain herself, 'Ooh. This is sooo exciting.'

Mary swivels around. 'Shut up. It's serious.'

'I told him about you. He said you should come.'

'I've gotta ask me mum and dad. I can't ...'

Dolly interrupts, 'Speaking of your dad, we betta get going.' Then, turning to you, 'What time do you have to be there?'

'Huh? Oh, six, six-thirty.'

'I can take you in if Mary is going. Where is it?'

'I don't ... he's at the Menzies? Do you know it?'

Dolly shrugs. 'I got a *Gregory's*. We'll find it. C'mon Mary, let's go ask.'

She remains still, giving a slight shake of the head. 'I can't. It's too ... my hair, and I've got nuthin' to wear.'

Taking her hand, 'Don't go to any trouble.'

Dolly laughs. 'I'll make you beautiful.'

Mary kisses you and runs after Dolly. The van disappears around the corner. You drop your head. *Fuck. Why now?*

≠

Mary emerges from the van, her lime-green dress shimmering in the light. Her hair is coiled, like a soft-serve ice cream in a cone—the kind you buy from a Mr Whippy van. You keep this to yourself, however. You have on your best clothes—the cheesecloth shirt from the door-to-door salesman and the corduroy pants.

'Let's go,' Dolly yells.

You grin, hoping to see Terry, but he's not in the van. 'Where's Terry?' Dolly doesn't reply. Mary tilts her head sideways, her eyes speaking volumes.

Hands clasped you stare out the window as street after street goes by. *Will he insist I go back? What about Mary?* The car slows to a crawl, inching its way along George Street towards Wynyard and the Menzies Hotel. Trembling, tightening your hold on her hand.

She whispers, 'Tell me more about your father.'

'There's not much to tell.' You hesitate. *He hit me. Never showed affection or put an arm around me unless it was to threaten me.* Lamely, you say, 'He doesn't like me,' falling into silence. The van comes to a stop before Mary can ask any more questions. A dead weight rests in your chest as you get out of the van. 'Thanks for the lift, Dolly.'

'I can come back and get you. I wanna hear all about it.'

Mary gives her a stern look, but you smile. 'We're gonna catch the train.' The van rattles as it pulls away, leaving the familiar trail of smoke. You chuckle. 'That fuckin' thing will fall apart one day.'

There's a sniff from behind. Turning around, a man in a red coat and matching pants faces you. A hand in a spotless white glove rubs his chin, a disparaging look on his face. 'Can I help you? Are you lost?' His words are clipped and formal.

You inhale. 'Umm, we're, we're meeting someone.'

He turns on his heel, stalks to the hotel entrance and takes hold of a brass handle, pulling the door open. 'Welcome to the Menzies.' He doesn't sound like he means it.

The entrance foyer shines with polished marble and gleaming brass. Men dressed in identical uniforms to the man outside, hurriedly scurry across the reception area. A few maneuver trolleys loaded with suitcases. You go unnoticed. Mary, directs your attention to a wall sign.

'The elevators are in that direction. Which floor is he on?'

Shrugging, 'I don't know.'

'Didn't you ask?'

'No. We can leave if ...'

She rolls her eyes. 'Stop it. C'mon, let's find out.'

Shuffling a stack of papers, a man behind the counter lifts his head. There's an audible sigh of frustration when Mary asks what floor room four two seven is on. 'Fourth floor, madam,' he responds in a manner the same as the man outside. You whisper into her ear that the hotel must teach them all to speak the same way. She suppresses a giggle, earning an irritated glance from the man.

With a thud, the elevator doors slide closed. Mary's fingertip presses 4 on the brass keypad before she absentmindedly twirls a strand of hair around her fingers—a gesture that mirrors your nervousness. A jolt as the elevator comes to a stop. The doors open.

Before you, room 427, you stare at the door as if it is the entrance, the source of all of your unease. *Will he be angry?*

Poised ready to knock, a wave of dread washes over you, momentarily freezing your hand. Your heart thunders so hard within your chest that you think it will break free. *I can't do this.* The fear is stifling. The feeling of wanting to collapse onto the ground and coil into a ball engulfs you. Pine aroma fills your nostrils. Toy helicopters, broken, lie among the pine needles. Your knees waver, one leg twitches as if struck—a solitary tear slides down your cheek. *No.*

Mary whispers in your ear, 'It's okay.'

For you, this moment signifies something entirely different—fear courses through you at the prospect of revisiting the past, uncertain if you can muster the strength to face him. *All you want is to know why?* Summoning a deep breath, you steady your racing heart and compose yourself, then knock. The door opens.

There's a warm smile on his face as he embraces Mary, then reaches for your hand. His once-dark hair has now turned a shade greyer. His shirt sleeves are rolled up, unusual as he is careful about his appearance. This seems out of character. He steps to the side. His eyes shifted between Mary and yourself. He dotes on her, pulling out a chair by a table near a window. Pouring her a glass of water, the ice-clinking resonates in the still air, she thanks him with a smile. Her eyes lock with yours over the rim of the glass before she places it down, a trace of red lipstick marking the edge. Your father, his smile taut, shifts his attention to you.

Your palms are moist. Wiping them on your thighs stains your corduroys. A metallic taste lingers at the back of your throat. *Is he about to?*

You stroll to a George Street restaurant with dark, Spanish-style furnishings. The embroidered fabric chairs require both hands to move them—a flickering candle in the table's centre is encircled by plastic flowers. A stout woman wipes sweat from her forehead and approaches with menus.

The weight of anticipation surrounds you. Recognising that Mary is a shield between you and him provides little solace. He directs his attention toward her, asking about her job, Sydney, and family. He avoids questions about you and her.

As the robust woman clears the dishes, he reclines, retrieving a pack of Benson & Hedges from a pocket, lighting up without extending one to you.

You wait. *Is he coming to the question that's hung between us all night?* The saying, 'tension you can cut with a knife' has never held much belief for you. However, tonight, it rings true.

His eyes probe yours. 'Your mum misses you. She'd like you to come back.'

There, he said it. What now? You hesitate, aware he didn't say home. Anger bubbles, and you want to scream. *Why? Why didn't you love me?* Instead, you mumble pitifully, 'I've, I've got work here.'

The veneer slips, a flash of annoyance on his face. 'You can get a job in Darwin.' With a deep breath, controlling himself, the veneer back, he persists. 'Your mum worries.'

'Um, I ... I don't think so.' The image of a young, frightened boy enters your thoughts. You find it difficult to suppress the emotions stirred by the memory of that five-year-old. Sensations well up in your throat, making you feel sick. There's one thing you're sure of: *He'll never lay another fuckin' hand on me.* Stammering, 'We, we must go, or .... or we'll miss our train.'

'Wait. I'll arrange a taxi.' He hurries away, you imagine relieved to remove himself. A man behind the counter nods, picking up a phone.

Mary leans closer. 'It's alright.' Her hand on your leg. You don't, you can't acknowledge her, and you stare at the candle as it finally sputters out.

He comes back at a slower pace. 'They'll arrange a taxi. It'll be about ten minutes.'

Standing in uneasy silence on George Street, a gentle drizzle begins, adding to the sombre mood. There are no words to bridge the gap. You have nothing to say to him. Throughout the night you sought fitting words, even striving for something light-hearted, yet your mind kept echoing the question: *Why?*

'Nice meeting you Mary,' he says as the taxi arrives, kissing her on the cheek and opening the rear door. He hands you money, holds onto your arm for a moment. 'Don't leave it too long.'

You walk to the other side of the taxi. 'Thanks for dinner.'

Mary takes your hand as the taxi moves away, her nails pressing into your palm. You wince but let out a relieved sigh. 'Thank goodness that's over.'

A smile curves on her lips. 'He's nice.'

You shrug, aware that she likely won't understand the depth of your fear and hate. Yes, finally, *you've said it, HATE*. Taking a deep breath. *How could she?*

The remainder of the journey passes in silence, your hand remains nestled in hers. As the taxi stops in front of her house, you give her a goodbye kiss on the cheek. You stop, surprised. Her makeup is smudged, tears on her cheeks, and in a choked voice, she stammers, 'What, what now?'

You forgot how this might affect her. 'I'm not sure... I mean, I haven't figured it out yet...'

She exits the taxi and gives a feeble smile before turning and retreating into her house.

≠

Betty is waiting—arms crossed over her ample bosom. There are no pleasantries, only a blunt, 'Well?'

'Shit, you scared me ... sorry ... I uh ...'

'How did it go?'

'He liked Mary.'

'And?'

Shaking your head, 'There's Mary.' It's all you can say as an overwhelming tiredness engulfs you.

She snaps, 'Excuses.' Stomping to her room, banging the door closed.

Kevin is also awake, and whispers—or his version of a whisper. 'You gonna go?'

Doesn't anyone sleep here? You don't, can't answer. Removing your clothes and climbing into bed, you stare at the ceiling, knowing there's to be no sleep tonight. Kevin's snores reverberate in the room, your heart races with doubt. The choice looms, *stay or go?* You give up on sleep and step outside, a wistful grin as memories resurface of your previous late-night roaming within the house. Uncertain of what to do, knowing that returning home will pose challenges, after all, leopards rarely change their spots.

The moon emerges from behind the clouds, a smile at the recollection of a similar moonlit night with Neal in the lounge room. A pang of sorrow at his absence. Determined, you turn on your heel to return inside, the path forward clearer in your mind.

≠

As you huddle together, battling the cold of the late afternoon. Mary quivers, drawing her jacket closer, brushing away a tear while sobs convulse her. Both of you are reluctant to voice the other's fear. You steal a glance. Her face is drained of happiness. Drawing nearer to her, she shudders.

'You'll find someone else. I know you will.'

'I won't go.'

'That's stupid. You have to.'

'Will you come with me?'

'I can't. My parents.' Groaning, 'Damn, here's the bus.'

'There'll be another. Stay. Please.'

Mary, with a washed-out smile. 'That's the third one. I've gotta go soon.' The bus slows, she absently waves it away. The horn toots as the vehicle gains speed, diesel fumes in its wake.

'Would you?'

Shaking her head, 'I don't know.' She stares after the disappearing bus. 'You and your dad need to sort things out.'

'Shit. I'm not sure about that.'

'You'll forget about me once you get back.'

Pulling her closer, whispering, 'I won't. I promise.'

≠

The morning that you are to leave arrives. Surprised at your air of calm as you prepare to go. Slipping into jeans and a T-shirt, you reflect on how Betty provided you with a safe harbour, a sense of being part of something. Memories of what you'll leave behind and those you'll gladly forget come to you: Kevin's farting, George's bravado, and Terry's consistent complaining are some of those you can do without. With a sigh, you contemplate the changes that have occurred in you, inconceivable twelve months ago. *But can I maintain who I am under his influence?*

In the kitchen, you discover Betty attacking the contents of a saucepan with gusto. Pausing, she lifts her arm, sniffs, and wipes her nose.

'You okay?'

Her back to you. 'I'm fine. A head cold.' She continues stirring the contents on the stove, her back wobbles.

'I, thanks for ...'

She interrupts. 'Yes, yes. Take care. I can't say I'll miss the racket you and Kevin made.'

You grin. 'Thanks for everything, and for taking a chance with me.' You swallow. 'I don't know what might have happened, if you ...'

She turns around, flushed from the heat of the stove or something else, a smile at the corner of her mouth. 'That first week,' she says, the words catching in her throat, she coughs, 'When you missed paying rent ...' She shakes her head, an unruly strand falling from under her scarf, then she turns back to the stove.

You stroll down the hallway, your nose wrinkling in response to the musty odour of mildew in the air. Oddly enough, you didn't recognise it when you first arrived. Since that first day, you overlooked everything, the wallpaper peeling at the edges and the cobwebs in the corners.

Now, the house is unmistakably weary. Your time here has reached its end.

You poke your head into Alfie's room, discovering him on his bed, muttering. With a parting wave, you leave him to his thoughts. Kevin and Des cross your path in the hallway. Des averts his eyes, and Kevin's face lights up with a grin. 'Big day.' A punch on your arm, followed by an embrace. George is fast asleep. Terry has been gone for days—Betty refused to take anyone else in after Peter's death.

A car horn blasts as Betty comes into the hallway. 'They'll break that thing if they're not careful.' She wraps you in a bear hug. 'There's always a bed. Even if I've gotta throw one of the others out.'

Your lips quiver. 'Tha ... Thanks.'

'Go on, or they'll leave without you.' She gives you a peck on the cheek and a reassuring pat before hurrying back to the kitchen. The horn sounds once more. Stepping out through the front door, you cast one last look at the house as you walk away.

≠

'Hurry up or you'll miss the fucking plane,' Terry shouts, hanging out of the passenger window. Mary rests against the side of the van, throwing your arms around her, without saying a word you both enter the rear. There are no posters on the roof.

The airport terminal is a bustling and bewildering place. Dolly points out a queue of people and tells you to check your bag. Handing the woman behind the counter your ticket, she stamps it and returns it to you with a smile. 'Boarding gate eleven. Have a pleasant flight.'

Mary tugs on your hand, urging you to follow her. 'Let's head this way,' she suggests, gesturing toward a window overlooking the tarmac, disregarding the comfortable looking lounge chairs. A plane taxies toward the terminal its Ansett logo reflects in the sunlight. Mary's grip on your hand tightens. Her racing heartbeat flows through your hands. You can't bring yourself to meet her gaze, so you stare out the window focusing on two men in yellow overalls maneuvering a set of stairs towards the now stationary aircraft. Passengers descend hurriedly, making their way from the stairs into the airport.

A whimper escapes Mary as a voice announces that boarding for flight nine two two to Darwin is now open. She hangs her head, squeezing your hand, mumbling, 'No.'

People shuffle past as you and Mary clutch each other both lost in your individual pain. A man fumbles with his briefcase, dropping it with a crash to the floor. A mother pushing a baby carriage stops, brushing back the hair from her tired face. You turn away from them, studying Mary, her shoulders slumped. You want to reassure her, to tell her it will be okay, but there are no words to ease her pain. Or at least, the ones you practice feel like a lie. Tears trickle down her cheeks. *What can I say?*

The anonymous voice announces final boarding for flight nine two two to Darwin.

Dolly yells, 'Graham, that's your plane.'

'Don't, don't cry. We'll see each other again.'

She shakes her head. 'I ...'

'We will. I'll call. And you've got the address.'

Dolly shouts again. 'C'mon or you'll miss it.'

Mary sobs. 'Go.'

'Not until you stop crying.'

Snuffling, wiping her nose, 'I'm okay. Go.'

You walk towards the boarding gate with a breaking heart. Dolly hugs you. 'Take care.'

'Thanks. Look after Mary.' She nods, sadness in her eyes.

Terry chuckles. 'Don't get into trouble.'

Smiling, 'If you're not around, I'll be fine.'

Kissing Mary, 'I'll miss you.' She nods, hiding her face in her hands.

In the queue, a young boy, filled with restless energy, wriggles within his father's grasp. The father releases his hold, allowing the boy to play on the floor. In the child's tiny hand, a toy helicopter, its metallic frame catching glimmers of light, its rotor blades whirring as it dances along the ground. The boy chortles, his laughter fills the air. Your mind trembles with memories of a different sight. You see another boy, accompanied by a father consumed by anger and self-loathing. A belt clenched in his hand; his face twisted with emotion not directed at you but at himself—a struggle he can't control.

A jolt pulls you back to the present. Someone is shaking your arm, their voice distant, lost in a confusing tunnel of thoughts. Mary's lips move, her face etched with concern. 'Is something wrong?' With a deep breath, calming yourself, you have nothing to say. The fight has begun.

Pressing your lips to hers, you turn away, striding down the corridor without a backward glance, head held high.

The End

About the Author

Graham Robinson was born in the United Kingdom, the second of four children. His family has lived in King's Lynn and Weston-super-Mare in England, Cape Town in South Africa, Windhoek in South-West Africa (now Namibia), and Perth and Darwin in Australia.

At thirteen, Graham left both home and school. By the 1980s, he had begun a career in radio as a broadcaster and journalist. In 2005, he moved to Canberra and joined the Australian Public Service. Graham has three children. *Pain, Loss & Desire* is his first book.

Acknowledgements

The completion of this book owes its existence to the invaluable support and guidance offered by writing coach and editor Paul Smitz. Paul undertook the challenge of supporting me to write a memoir.

Thanks also to Paula Diaco from *writestoriesnow* who emphasised the significance of delving into my childhood trauma.

I am grateful to author Denise Imwold, whose manuscript review provided insightful commentary—my appreciation to Linda Powell for her valuable advice, which contributed to shaping the book.

A special mention to those who recognised my past traumas and provided healing. Life coach Mary-Anne Quezel, whose guidance has been invaluable. Additionally, thanks to the Australian Chapter of Path Retreats, whose unwavering support provided a nurturing environment for confronting and addressing my trauma. The contribution of these individuals has been transformative, and it is to them I owe the fact that this book came into being and, more importantly, the person I am today.

www.ingramcontent.com/pod-product-compliance
Lightning Source LLC
Chambersburg PA
CBHW020314010526
44107CB00054B/1842